The God of Small Places

The God of Small Places

A Rural Church Institute Resource

EDITED BY
Glenn Daman AND
Jeffrey Clark

FOREWORD BY
Jason R. McConnell

WIPF & STOCK · Eugene, Oregon

THE GOD OF SMALL PLACES
A Rural Church Institute Resource

Wipf & Stock
An Imprint of Wipf and Stock Publishers
199 W. 8th Ave., Suite 3
Eugene, OR 97401

www.wipfandstock.com

PAPERBACK ISBN: 979-8-3852-6829-0
HARDCOVER ISBN: 979-8-3852-6830-6
EBOOK ISBN: 979-8-3852-6831-3

VERSION NUMBER 02/03/26

Contents

Foreword

AGAINST ALL ODDS, I became a follower of Jesus Christ and received a call to vocational ministry at Josephine Covenant Community Church—a small country parish with an average Sunday attendance of about forty-five people, rising to sixty on holidays. The church was nestled among the coal fields of Josephine, a tiny town in western Pennsylvania whose population fluctuated between two hundred and three hundred, depending on the number of tragic deaths recorded in the community since the last census. Remarkably, for a village without a traffic light and only two stop signs, it still managed to claim its own zip code and post office.

The church building was anything but impressive. Picture a weathered, single-story structure clad in dingy white vinyl siding, its identity announced by a crooked sign listing the name and service time. Inside, the sanctuary offered little charm. A cramped and cluttered space, outdated wood-paneled walls, and the carpet—an unfortunate shade of green—did nothing to disguise years of neglect. In one corner sat an upright piano, perpetually out of tune. The foyer was nothing more than a makeshift entryway, while the concrete-block cellar had been converted into a crude children's Sunday school room, complete with a dusty second-hand ping-pong table.

There were no stained-glass windows to lift the eyes toward transcendence—only water stains on the sagging drop ceiling, silent reminders of decay. The scene called to mind Charlie Brown's decrepit Christmas tree,[1] or more profoundly, the prophet's description of the suffering servant:

> He had no form or majesty that we should look at him. . . . He was despised and rejected by men, a man of sorrows and acquainted

1. Schulz, *Charlie Brown Christmas.*

> with grief; and as one from whom men hide their faces, he was despised, and we esteemed him not. There was no beauty that we should desire him. (Isa 53:2–3)

My school bus passed the church every day of my childhood, yet I hardly noticed it. Growing up in a completely secular family, I didn't know a single person who attended, nor did I have any idea what people actually did inside a church. My only frame of reference came from television shows like *Little House on the Prairie*, where an elderly pastor led a small flock in a few dreary hymns before delivering an old-fashioned religious lecture.[2]

Then, by a marvelous stroke of God's providence, I stumbled into that very church one Sunday morning during my junior year of high school—and my life was forever changed. In that humble sanctuary, I felt the presence of God. I heard a clear proclamation of the gospel of Jesus Christ and was gripped by its message of forgiveness and redemption. By then, I had already made choices that left me burdened with guilt and shame, shaped by tragedy, trauma, and generational sin. Yet this congregation offered the most compelling hope I had ever encountered. Despite its unimpressive appearance and lack of the usual markers of "successful" ministry, the people of Josephine Covenant embodied the gospel in both word and deed, making disciples with a faithfulness I have rarely seen since.

At the time, I didn't fully appreciate what God had done in directing me to that rural church—a community rooted in Scripture and committed to the Great Commission. They placed a Bible in my hands and patiently taught me how to read it. They welcomed me into their weekly men's prayer meeting, where I learned the powerful discipline of intercessory prayer. Families opened their homes to me, modeling Christian love and hospitality around their dinner tables.

Only six months after my conversion, my pastor looked me in the eye and said with deliberate, yet daunting confidence: "You've been walking with Jesus for a while now; it's probably time for you to preach your first sermon." From that moment, he began mentoring me in hermeneutics and homiletics, entrusting me with leadership in the youth ministry and guiding me toward the calling God had placed on my life. At first, I felt as though I was receiving special treatment, but I soon realized this was simply the culture of the church. Every member was expected to grow in their relationship with Christ and to use their spiritual gifts in service to

2. Hanalis, *Little House*.

others. Because this was my only experience of church life, I assumed such intentional discipleship was the norm everywhere.

At that time, I never imagined there might be a need for a theology of rural ministry. I simply believed that God was present everywhere, working in all places regardless of their size or cultural significance. When I first read the Gospel of John, I was puzzled by Nathaniel's dismissive response to Philip's announcement of the Messiah: "Can anything good come out of Nazareth?" (John 1:46). I didn't want to judge Nathaniel's skepticism, but I couldn't understand why Nazareth would be considered unworthy. To me, it seemed as fitting a place as any for the Messiah to come from. His reaction baffled me, since I had never encountered rural stigmatization. Growing up in a small community, I assumed his work was equally evident in large cities, sprawling suburbs, and tiny towns alike. It wasn't until I left home for college and began searching for a new church that I first came across urban and suburban elitism—and realized that my rural church was far more unique than I had ever recognized.

When I arrived in Chicago in the late 1990s, the upperclassmen in my dorm invited me to join them at church. I was eager to explore new expressions of Christian worship and to continue my apprenticeship under another pastor. I vividly recall visiting megachurches with hip names like Willow Creek Community Church, Rock of Our Salvation, and Harvest Bible Chapel—only to be struck by the unsettling reality that most congregants had no personal relationship with their pastor, let alone the opportunity to be mentored by him. I was also introduced to an array of compartmentalized clerical titles—executive pastor, outreach pastor, discipleship pastor, worship pastor, children's pastor, next gen pastor—a taxonomy that still puzzles me today. It seemed odd that so many bore the title "pastor" yet devoted their time and energy to managing programs rather than proclaiming the gospel through word and sacrament. Quietly, I wondered: shouldn't every pastor be engaged in outreach and discipleship?

After spending several months immersed in the megachurch scene, I was both astonished and disillusioned to realize that this was the norm for so many American Christians. It was during this time that I first encountered what felt like a corporate ladder within the church. I was troubled to hear my Bible college classmates speak in careerist terms: "I hope I can land a pastoral internship at a big church so I can eventually take over as lead pastor," and "I'll probably need three to five years at a small congregation before I can move up to a larger one."

Although I lacked the spiritual knowledge and ecclesial experience to articulate a theology of rural ministry, I now clearly sensed the need for one. My desire was simple: to serve Jesus and to offer others what the Josephine Covenant Community Church had given me. I had no ambition to lead a megachurch or to pursue what many considered "successful" ministry. In Scripture, I never saw success defined by the size of a congregation, the amount of money collected, or the acreage of a church campus. Nor did I see the rural church as a mere stepping stone to something larger or more prestigious.

This conviction only deepened when I reflected on the story of Philip and the Ethiopian eunuch in Acts 8. God called Philip away from a thriving revival in Samaria—marked by miraculous healings, dramatic exorcisms, and incredible evangelistic fruit—and sent him instead to a barren rural road. When the angel of the Lord commanded, "Rise and go toward the south to the road that goes down from Jerusalem to Gaza" (Acts 8:26), Philip did not protest or lament what might have seemed like a ministry demotion. He simply obeyed, leaving a booming urban ministry in "a city in Samaria" (Acts 8:5) for what Luke describes as "a desert place" (Acts 8:26).

If ministry success were measured by numbers or visibility, Philip's decision would have made little sense. Or if he had read Henry Blackaby's book *Experiencing God*, which encourages people to watch "to see where God is at work" and "join Him in His work,"[3] he never would have left Samaria. Yet his obedience ensured that this solitary gentile was transformed by the gospel as it reached beyond the urban centers of "Jerusalem, Judea, and Samaria" to the rural roads at "the ends of the earth" (Acts 1:8)—a reminder that God's purposes are never bound by consumeristic notions of "bigger is better." If we are not able to see God working in a particular location, does it mean that he isn't present or working in profound ways? As depraved human beings, can we trust our eyes to perceive where or when or how or in whom God is working? Who would have guessed that God was about to do a great work on a remote dessert road in Gaza?

With these questions swirling in my soul, I began searching for a robust theology of rural ministry. I longed for an affirmation that the God who created the heavens and the earth cares as deeply for those who dwell in the countryside as much as those who reside on city streets. I needed help understanding why rural communities are often maligned by Christians, even though our Savior was born in the little town of Bethlehem, raised

3. Blackaby and King, *Experiencing God*, 78.

in nowhere Nazareth, and conducted most of his ministry among peasant fishing villages scattered around the Sea of Galilee. I hoped someone would acknowledge that my vocational aspiration of becoming a country parson was worthwhile, rather than dismissing it as second-class work for pastors who lacked the charisma to ascend the megachurch platform. Yet, despite my searching, I found little written on the subject.

During my undergraduate and graduate studies, particularly while completing my doctoral dissertation on rural and small church ministry, I read nearly every book on the topic published before 2010. Some were helpful, but many were not. Lyle Schaller's extensive writings on church size dynamics and leadership, published from the mid-1960s through the early 1990s, often felt formulaic and outdated. Works by Hartford Seminary professor Carl S. Dudley and American Baptist pastor Anthony Pappas, published through the Alban Institute, offered practical insights but lacked theological depth. As far as I could tell, one had to reach all the way back to George Herbert's *The Country Parson* (1652) to find a work on rural ministry with genuine theological gravitas.

In 1996, Ron Klassen and John Koessler published *No Little Places: The Untapped Potential of the Small Town Church*. It was the only modern book I found that offered any theological vision for rural ministry, though its brevity left me wanting more. Thankfully, the past decade has been more fruitful. Donnie Griggs's *Small Town Jesus: Taking the Gospel Mission Seriously in Seemingly Unimportant Places* (2016) marked the first significant attempt at a theology of rural ministry in twenty years. Brad Roth followed with his elegantly written *God's Country: Faith, Hope, and the Future of the Rural Church* (2017), and Stephen Witmer's *A Big Gospel in Small Places: Why Ministry in Forgotten Communities Matters* (2019) provided a seminal contribution. Each of these works has elevated the profile of rural ministry in the broader Christian community, pointing readers to the God who created all creatures—and all places—great and small.

Still, much work remains. That is why I am grateful for my friends Glenn Daman and Jeff Clark, who have joined forces as general editors to produce this present volume. They have assembled a remarkable team of rural pastor-theologians that represent a wide range of theological traditions, from Southern Baptist to Wesleyan and Nazarene—as well as diverse geographical contexts—from the cornfields of the Midwest to the coalfields of Appalachia, the evergreen forests of the Pacific Northwest, the prairies of Minnesota, and the arid grasslands of West Texas. Together, they help us understand the God of small places and his care for rural communities and people who inhabit them.

Glenn, a seasoned rural pastor and author of several of the finest books I have read on small church ministry, brings vast pastoral wisdom. Jeff, a gifted rural church planter, global researcher, and missiologist with the International Mission Board of the Southern Baptist Convention, also served as my predecessor as director of the Rural Church Institute at the Wheaton College Billy Graham Center. Both possess the theological depth and sociological insight needed to guide this collaborative effort. Through their leadership, the authors highlight theological perspectives on rural communities, rural ministry, the rural church, and the rural pastor. By weaving together biblical, systematic, and pastoral theology, they create a rich tapestry that reveals the mission of gospel and the beauty of redemption in small places.

Just as Captain Meriwether Lewis and Lieutenant William Clark once led the Corps of Discovery in pursuit of treasures beyond the Northwest Passage, Daman and Clark—along with an exceptional lineup of rural church leaders—now chart a different kind of expedition. With biblical precision and theological conviction, they guide us to rise above the mountains of American pragmatism and to navigate the perilous waters of suburban superiority, uncovering the treasures of God that remain hidden in rural obscurity.

Therefore, whether you are already a rural church leader, a college or seminary student discerning a call to rural ministry, an urban or suburban pastor considering a transition to a country parish, or simply someone whom the Holy Spirit has stirred with curiosity about this work, I gladly commend this volume to you. My prayer is that you will find the journey as enriching and joyful as I did.

And finally, this book is proudly published under the auspices of the Rural Church Institute at the Wheaton College Billy Graham Center. It is part of the Institute's ongoing mission to strengthen, equip, and encourage rural congregations and their leaders. By situating this work within that larger vision, my hope is that it will serve not only as a personal reflection but also as a resource that contributes to the flourishing of rural ministry across the wider church.

Dr. Jason R. McConnell
Director of the Rural Church Institute
at the Wheaton College Billy Graham Center
December 2025

Contributors

Glenn Daman (DMin, Trinity Evangelical Divinity School) has served for over thirty-five years as a pastor of rural churches in Montana, Oregon, and Washington. He also serves on the Board of Directors of Village Missions. He has written numerous articles and five books on rural and small-church ministry: *Leading the Small Church*, *Shepherding the Small Church*, *Developing Leaders for the Small Church*, *When Shepherds Weep*, and *The Forgotten Church*. He is co-author (with Jeff Clark) of the book *Retooling the Rural Church for the 21st Century* (forthcoming). He grew up on a farm in northern Idaho. Glenn is married to Becky, and they have two married children. He enjoys photography, woodworking, camping with his family, and spending time working on the family farm.

John Adams (DMin, Western Seminary) is the executive director of Village Missions and has twenty-one years of rural church ministry experience. John's formative years were on a rural farm in central Idaho, where he and his family attended the only church. John is married to Candy, a Village Missionary's daughter, and they have two married children. He enjoys hiking, swimming, woodworking, and spending time with family.

Rex J. Howe (ThM, Dallas Theological Seminary) is currently a postgraduate research student at the University of Aberdeen, Scotland, in the School of Divinity, History, and Philosophy. His research focuses on the *nomina sacra* in early Christian manuscripts and pneumatology. Rex has enjoyed serving local churches in Minford, Ohio, as a youth pastor at Fairview Missionary Baptist Church (2003–2007); in Dallas, Texas, as an assistant pastor of youth and outreach at Scofield Church (2007–2015); and in Lisbon, Illinois, as senior pastor of West Lisbon Church (2015–2020). He now serves as the sixth president of Tri-State Bible College. He is married to Aimee, and the couple has three children. Together, they worship as members of Wheelersburg Baptist Church, where they serve in the children's ministry.

Jonathan Hansen (MEd, University of Nebraska) is director of missionary development at Village Missions. In 1996, Jon and his wife, Debbie, joined Village Missions. They spent fourteen years shepherding rural churches in Nebraska and Kansas and then served as district representatives. In 2020, Jon began serving as the assistant director of Village Missions and currently serves as director of missionary development. He worked in education for seventeen years before becoming a Village Missionary. Jon has been married to Debbie for thirty-five years, and they have one daughter, Hannah, who is married to her husband, Luke.

Charles E. Cotherman (PhD, University of Virginia) is executive director of the Center for Rural Ministry and assistant professor of biblical and theological studies at Grove City College. He has served in numerous pastoral and para-church ministry roles and has over ten years of experience in rural ministry. He is the lead pastor of Oil City Vineyard Church, a church he and his wife planted in 2016 in Oil City, Pennsylvania. He has published widely on topics including religious history, church planting, and rural ministry. His books include *Sent to Flourish: A Guide to Planting and Multiplying Churches* (IVP Academic), of which he was a contributor and co-editor, and *To Think Christianly: A History of L'Abri, Regent College, and the Christian Study Center Movement* (IVP Academic).

Ron Klassen (DMin, Bethel Seminary) is director emeritus of the Rural Home Missionary Association (RHMA). He served as the executive director of RHMA from 1990–2023. He has been a frequent conference speaker and a guest professor at a number of Bible colleges, universities, and seminaries, and is an adjunct professor at Dallas Theological Seminary. He has written dozens of articles, including several for *Leadership Journal*. Ron is the author of *Maximize! Leveraging the Strengths of Your Small Church*. He has co-authored two books: *No Little Places: The Untapped Potential of the Small-Town Church* and *Leading Through Change: Shepherding the Town and Country Church in a New Era*. Ron has been married to Roxy since 1977. They have been blessed with three children, a daughter- and son-in-law, and two granddaughters.

Rob Beckett is a pastor, author, and director of The Revitalization Network (engaging, equipping, and empowering pastors to help their churches transform the community). He received the Kentucky District of the Nazarene Go Award, presented for outstanding service advancing missions, and the WLKY Bell Award for outstanding humanitarian efforts of local volunteers in Metro Louisville. Rob pastors a church that was declining and dying; this church now serves as a hub to the community as a viable and transforming part of Shepherdsville and the surrounding county. He has co-written several books on church revitalization, including *God's Pattern for Revitalization* and *Fanning the Revitalization Flame: Leading Your Church from Smoldering Embers to Revival Fire*. Rob is married to Joanna, and they have three grown children and a grandson.

Kyle Bueermann (DMin, Rockbridge Seminary) serves as a rural specialist with the North American Mission Board's Replant team. He served as a pastor in New Mexico for almost nine years, and as a youth and music pastor at several churches in West Texas prior to that. Kyle has co-hosted the popular weekly podcast *Not Another Baptist Podcast* from 2017–2024. He's the author of *They Devoted Themselves* and the co-author of *Replanting Rural Churches* (with Matt Henslee). He is married to Michelle, and they have two kids, Noah and Hailey. Kyle is an avid reader, loves black coffee, and is a die-hard fan of the Texas Rangers baseball club. Kyle and his family live in Lubbock, Texas.

Martin Giese (DMin, Bethel Theological Seminary) serves as president of Oak Hills Christian College and the Oak Hills Fellowship (Oak Hills Christian College, Camp Oak Hills, Oak Hills Center for Native American Ministries, and Oak Hills Church Ministries) in Bemidji, Minnesota. Previously, Martin served for seventeen years as pastor of First Baptist Church of Parkers Prairie, Minnesota, and twenty-three years as senior pastor of Faithbridge Church of Park Rapids, Minnesota. Martin served for ten years as an adjunct faculty member of the Billy Graham School of Evangelism, instructing on evangelism for town and country churches. Martin also served as founder and director of the Country Shepherds' Workshop at Oak Hills Christian College. Martin is a conference speaker and consultant on town and country church leadership. Martin grew up on a farm in western Minnesota (Appleton) and enjoys family events, hunting, fishing, reading, and landscaping. Martin and his wife, Marcia, have four children—Anna (Shane) Long, Sarah (Jeff) Donatelle, Rachel Giese, and David (Sally) Giese—thirteen grandchildren, and two step-grandchildren.

TJ Freeman spent his childhood dreaming of the day he could leave small-town Pennsylvania behind. After earning a degree in education (Cedarville University), he taught high school social studies and coached soccer until an opportunity came to help plant a church in a growing southwest Florida city. TJ has served as the senior pastor of Christ Church since 2012. He is a founding board member of The Brainerd Institute, a resource to equip men for rural ministry through pastoral residency, conferences, articles, and a podcast. TJ enjoys backpacking and photography and prefers temperatures above eighty degrees. He is married to his high school sweetheart, Katie, and they have four children: Charlotte, Charity, Hudson, and Grant.

John Hindley is the pastor of Broadgrace Church in the village of Coltishall in the rural east of England. He has served there since leading the team the Lord used to plant the church in 2010. Alongside serving as a rural pastor, John has written a number of books that address the challenges, discouragements, and sufferings that impact Christians, including *Serving Without Sinking*, *Dealing with Disappointment*, and *You Can Really Grow*. His most recent book, *Weakness Our Strength*, grew out of reflecting on the comparative weakness of many rural churches and the design of Christ in this discouragement, and other areas of weakness. John has also published a book of vacation devotions, *Refreshed*, from his time spent in creation as a rural pastor. John has also written a curriculum on rural ministry for Crosslands. John is married to Felicity, and they have four children ranging from preschool to high school. He enjoys family life, reading, and any excuse to get out his tools and work on a project.

J. Matthew Shamblin (PhD, Tennessee Temple University) is currently senior pastor at Rose Hill Baptist Church in Ashland, Kentucky. He has pastored churches in Virginia, West Virginia, and Kentucky. He is interested in the study of Appalachia, leadership, biblical studies, and adoption. He also serves as a professor at Tri-State Bible College, South Point, Ohio, where he is the Appalachian research fellow. He teaches both undergraduate and graduate courses and is co-host of the *Level Paths* podcast. A native of West Virginia, Matt is married and the father of two.

Kevin Blackwell (DMin, New Orleans Baptist Theological Seminary, PhD, Midwestern Baptist Theological Seminary) is the executive director of the Mobile Baptist Network in Mobile, Alabama. He also serves as assistant professor of disciple making and special assistant to the president at the

University of Mobile. Married for thirty years with four children, he lives in Alabama. Experienced pastor and church leader, he was awarded the prestigious Troy L. Morrison Award for pastoral leadership by the Alabama Baptist Convention in 2011. He is a former president of the Alabama Baptist Pastor's Conference (2014). His dissertation thesis was "An Analysis and Critique of Disciple Making Within Ecclesial Movements in the United States, 1970–2020, with a View Toward Implementing a Faithful New Testament *Missio Ecclesia*." He is an avid runner, passionate sports fan, and proponent of a biblical worldview.

Jeff Clark (DMin, Southern Baptist Theological Seminary) and his wife started churches in remote northern Michigan, the suburbs of Orlando, and rural middle Tennessee. Then, Jeff served the West Virginia Convention of Southern Baptists, overseeing church planting and evangelism. Afterward, he became the executive director of the Montana Southern Baptist Convention. For thirteen years, the Clarks served in East Asia doing research, evangelism, and training rural church planters. They currently live in Richmond, Virginia, and Jeff serves as a director for Wheaton College Billy Graham Center's Rural Church Institute and as the rural mobilizer for the International Mission Board. He is the co-author (with Glenn Daman) of the book *Retooling the Rural Church for the 21st Century* (forthcoming).

Introduction

Developing a Theological Foundation

Glenn Daman

At age twelve, sitting in the back of a small rural church in northern Idaho and listening to a missionary share his stories about reaching people on the island of Borneo (also known as Kalimantan), I sensed God's calling to ministry. It was not dramatic. No audible voice, no overpowering presence of the Holy Spirit. It was a deep awareness that God had called me to serve him. After completing seminary, my wife and I loaded the U-Haul and journeyed to a small town in eastern Montana to begin our first pastoral ministry. I was eager to proclaim God's word to the people in this rural church, helping them grow in their knowledge of the Bible, doctrine, and godly living. What started as a brief foray into rural ministry became a lifelong calling.

Shortly after we arrived, I received a call from desperate parents of a teen having an emotional breakdown and needing someone to counsel the family. The nearest mental health counselor was over 250 miles away, so they called me instead. I had no idea what to do or say when I arrived at their home. As I entered their house, I distinctly remember reflecting upon my studies in seminary and thinking, "How does eschatology relate to this?" I was prepared to teach people about the depths of our theology and the richness of the biblical text. But I was not ready to help a family in an emotional crisis. Thus, I was confronted with a struggle we all face in ministry: is the theology we learned in seminary relevant to people's daily lives, or is it merely applicable for theological navel-gazing?

Yet the question goes deeper than providing counsel to people in a crisis. It goes to the heart of ministry. Graduating from seminary gives us the tools to refute theological error and properly exegete the text, but what about the daily struggles of life and ministry? Sometimes, we marvel that God has given us the privilege of serving him by ministering to his people. Other times, we feel our call is a curse rather than a blessing. We struggle to understand why church attendance is declining and our community remains unresponsive to the gospel. As we confront the issues and challenges of ministry, we question the relevance of our theological training.

For Paul, theology was more than just affirming biblical doctrines about God and salvation. Theology is the fabric of life and the foundation for ministry. Rather than theology being disconnected from life and ministry, Paul places it at the center. When Paul wrote to Timothy and Titus, young men starting in ministry, he did not stress the importance of programs and methods. Instead, he emphasized the centrality of doctrine to their ministry. Doctrine was not just the content of their teaching, it was the basis for godly living and practice (see 1 Tim 4:6; 6:3; 2 Tim 4:3; Titus 1:9; 2:7). Paul encourages Titus to be an example to younger men of purity in doctrine (Titus 1:7) and to teach bondslaves to "adorn the doctrine of God our Savior in every respect" (Titus 1:9). Theology was not just theoretical statements, but transformational truths. Yet, as we read Paul's writing, we struggle with the questions: How does our theology provide the basis for effective ministry in rural communities? How does our theology guide and direct us in leading the church and interacting with the community? How does our theology answer the most challenging problems confronting our ministry, our lives, and the people in the pews?

As pastors, we are often the ultimate pragmatists. Books focusing on "how to" fill the shelves of pastors' libraries. We devour books that instruct us how to grow the church, organize the church, deal with conflict, do evangelism . . . and the list goes on. The last thing pastors think they need or want is a book on theology. The lack of time due to busy schedules is compounded for pastors in rural settings, where the pastor is often the only staff member and may have a second job. Such a pastor has precious little time to read a book on the theological foundation for ministry.

The danger in focusing on the "how to" books to the exclusion of the "why" books is that rural leaders can substitute the "what works" for the "why." The risk comes from not examining whether the "what works" aligns with the "why" from Scripture. It is this question that makes us look to our theology.

We now live in a world that has undergone radical changes over the last fifty years. What worked in rural churches in 1975 no longer works in rural churches today. Before turning to the internet to find the latest book on how to grow a church in suburbia, we first need a theological foundation for rural ministry, in which our theology not only shapes our doctrinal statement but also shapes everything we do in ministry. Then, from this foundation, we develop biblically sound strategies that are manifested in the ministries of the local church within their local community.

Developing a Theology for Rural Ministry

How do we navigate a world where the methods we learned in seminary regarding ministry no longer work? How do we minister in a postmodern culture now prevalent in rural communities? The answer lies in the pages of Scripture. The Bible remains relevant because it was inspired by a God who knows all people, in all cultures, at all times, and the Bible is intended to be relevant to all people, cultures, and times.

When we think of theology, we often think of our days in seminary studying the nuances of the Greek text and its implications for understanding the debate regarding God's sovereign election and man's free will. Too often, theology is taught in an abstract and theoretical manner rather than in a practical and relevant one. We distinguish between systematic theology (what we believe) and practical theology (how we lead a church) as if the two are disconnected. As a result, we see the Bible as a textbook but the church as a business. We believe that success in ministry comes by incorporating the latest programs and methods that have achieved growth in a large urban church, rather than reflecting deeply upon our theology and how it guides our lives and ministry.

The Necessity for a Theological Foundation for Our Ministry

For Paul, the starting point in navigating our confusing world is to develop a robust theology that provides the basis and motivation for all we do within the church. Theology not only governs what we believe but also how and why we do what we do in ministry. The greatest danger confronting the church today is not irrelevant or ineffective programs, it is the failure to have a ministry theologically grounded (2 Tim 4:2–3). Our theology provides us with everything we need for ministry (2 Tim 3:16–17; Titus 2:10). Effectiveness in ministry begins by incorporating our theology into every facet of church life.

This theological foundation is not only necessary for developing a healthy church but also critical for transforming people. We must translate what the Bible teaches about God into the culture, language, and life of the people we serve. Within God's character and his goal for humanity, we discover the foundation for the church's teaching, the goal of our ministry, and the basis by which we measure our success. Our theology provides the lens through which we view our culture, the connecting tissue that binds the ministries together, and the end we strive to attain. To integrate our theology into ministry, we must move it from the ivory towers of seminary with its abstract language into the lives and language of the local mechanic, farmer, rancher, factory worker, and housewife. Otherwise, we become irrelevant to our community, no longer having biblical answers to people's challenges. The Bible becomes an ancient record rather than the living word of God, transforming people and communities.

At the core of our theology is the unchanging mission of God to reach the world with the gospel of Christ. This mission undergirds everything we do in ministry. It is the overarching plan that governs and dictates all other programs and ministries in the church. We must maintain a focused, shared missional purpose, determined by our theology, which serves as the basis for all decisions made within the church. Bolsinger rightly points out, "The first question about leading into uncharted territory is not about change but what will *not* change. So first, we determine what is precious, what is worth keeping no matter the circumstances, what will never change, what is the core ideology of the church."[1] This mission, grounded in God's redemptive plan and derived from our understanding of God's character, governs everything we do within the church. Consequently, our theology will have a greater significant impact on the future health of the church than all the church's programs and strategies.[2]

Second, a theological foundation for the rural church necessitates a clear understanding and formation of our doctrines, creeds, and concrete statements that describe God's nature and our relationship with him within

1. Bolsinger, *Canoeing the Mountains*,128.

2. See Daman, *Shepherding the Small Church*, 65–84.

the context of a rural church. Theology begins with the orderly arrangement of coherent statements of beliefs. Without such statements, we are prey to the infiltration of false doctrines that undermine our faith and destroy our lives. However, these statements are not just doctrinal confessions but truths that form the foundation of our values, ethics, and understanding of God. They are the unchanging teachings of Scripture, upon which we build a consistent worldview, and are the basis for the core teachings that govern the church. If we do not know what we believe, we will not know how to live and minister effectively in a complex and confusing world.

Lastly, we must bridge the gap between what the Bible says about God and how we respond to the everyday realities of life. Doctrinal statements are of little value if they do not serve as our guide in ministry. When Paul spoke to the Jews and the Greeks, the mission and content of the gospel message remained unchanged. *How* he communicated the gospel radically shifted to connect with the individuals based on their culture and background. Paul's adaptation reminds us that all ministry is cross-cultural because every community and every church has its own culture. A rural community in New England is culturally different from a ranching community in North Dakota. An African American church in the Deep South differs from an Indigenous church on a reservation in Arizona. Each of these communities faces different struggles and challenges in their personal lives, churches, and communities. As pastors, our task is to provide the bridge between what the Bible says about God (theology) and what our people are facing (praxis).

This gap between our theology and the daily ministry of the church is what Tim Keller describes as the "'middle space' between doctrine and practice—a 'space where we reflect deeply on our theology and culture to understand how both of them shape our ministry.'"[3] Our integration of theology in our ministry enables us to connect the doctrines of the Bible to our local church and community by allowing us to see our life and ministry through the lens of Scripture. This requires that we be fluent in both our theology and localized culture to recognize where the gospel alternately challenges and affirms them. As David Clark points out, "Theological reflection properly includes not just thought, but life. It involves not just cognition, but spirituality (formation and inner transformation) and behavior (obedience to Christ and service to the world)."[4] It is one thing to

3. Witmer, "Five Ways," 104.

4. Clark, *To Know and Love God*, 113–14.

affirm the sovereignty of God, but how does the sovereignty of God bring hope to a church struggling with the threat of closing? How does it comfort someone who lost a child in a tragic accident? How does it provide peace for a local store owner on the brink of bankruptcy because Walmart has opened a superstore in the next town? As leaders, we must move theology from the language of theology books to the language and struggles of the people we serve. Effectiveness in ministry is not measured by the numbers in the pews but by the transformation of people as they conform their lives to the person and purpose of God. This begins by reflecting deeply on our theology and explaining how it relates to a farmer facing foreclosure or a church struggling in a dying village.

The Process of Developing a Theological Foundation for Rural Ministry

Developing a theological foundation involves a dialogue between what we believe about God, the challenges we face in ministry, and the people we serve within the local community. This dialogue begins by first connecting with our local community to understand its culture and identify areas of cultural and theological congruence between our theology and the community's local culture and ethos. In so doing, we establish a basis for connecting the gospel to their world. All cultures have levels of agreement with Scripture, where their culture reflects, illustrates, and clarifies biblical truth. Finding commonality between the Bible and their world and communicating those connections within the language, symbols, and stories of the people we serve provides the basis for becoming relevant to them. When Paul first addressed the philosophers on Mars Hill, he did not start by confronting their false idolatry. Instead, he began by linking with their world (Acts 17:22). By discovering these connections, we can bridge our message with their world. Before they will listen to us, we need to listen to them. They must know we accept them and are willing to enter their world. By doing so, we earn their trust, without which they will reject us and our message.

Second, to engage our local culture, we need to contextualize our theology and the gospel by relating and communicating the gospel within the language and culture of our community. The way people relate to one another, the values they hold, the language and stories they use to communicate these shared values, the music they listen to, and even their cultural expectations of the church vary from community to community.

For example, the language and culture of a logging community differ significantly from those of a farming community. The values of a New England village differ from those in the Northern Plains. These differences are expressed in their language, the yarns they share at the local coffee shop, and the debates within the local politics. Paul understood the importance of contextualization when he becomes all things to all men to win some (1 Cor 9:19–23). This is true within the community as well as within the local church. As pastors, we need to become historians of both; that is, we learn the history of the community we serve and become champions of that history, communicating the gospel in a way they can understand and connect with.

Third, we must relate our theology to the community's issues and the people's lives. People do not care about what we believe until they see how it answers their daily struggles. When Christ confronted the woman at the well, he did not start with a theological discussion of Jewish and Samaritan theology. Instead, he began with a discussion about water. By relating the gospel to her immediate need for water, he contextualized it for her life. He connected his message to her broken life marked by multiple marriages. By doing so, he could address her need for spiritual transformation. If our message is unconnected to their world and irrelevant to them, they will never listen to what we have to say.

Fourth, we must transform their culture by identifying and correcting those areas of their culture and social structures that violate the gospel. Theological engagement involves examining local beliefs, values, and patterns in light of the truths of Scripture to transform one's view of God and confront cultural biases that distort their understanding of Scripture. We must not only answer their questions but also change the framework within which they are asked. As Richard Lints points out, "A theological vision allows [people] to see their culture in a way different than they had ever been able to see it before. . . . Those who are empowered by the theological vision do not simply stand against the mainstream impulses of the culture but take the initiative to both understand and speak to that culture from the framework of Scripture. The modern theological vision must seek to bring the entire counsel of God into the world if its time so that its time might be transformed."[5]

Last, theological engagement seeks to learn from the local culture. Each of us has cultural biases that cloud our perspective. Therefore, as we

5. Keller, *Center Church*, 18; brackets original.

enter a dialogue with the people we serve, we not only correct false beliefs, but they can also give us insight that confronts our misconceptions. In the process, we gain a deeper understanding of Scripture. For example, a farmer's reading of the parables of the kingdom in Matt 13 can provide insight beyond a mere grammatical study of Greek. It helps to bridge a modernized, urbanized culture to the agrarian culture of the first-century Jews to whom Jesus was connecting. In this interaction, we also gain new insight into Scripture regarding the attitude of the farmer (God) and his relationship and connection with the harvest.

When we develop a theological foundation for rural ministry, we present the gospel to people in a way they can understand and relate to, so that they are transformed by it. Therefore, we must not only become engaged with the rural culture to gain acceptance, but it is also necessary to transform them through the application of the Bible to their lives.

The Nature and Activity of God: The Foundation for Theology

Ecclesiastes is a book of theological reflection as Solomon seeks to apply the lessons of wisdom to the real and broken world in which he lived. After examining his culture and its values (pleasure, success, wealth, power, etc.), he concluded that it was all a vaporless mist. Like a cloud, it has substance but lacks weight or eternal value. It is not that these things are necessarily evil in themselves (although their misuse may lead to evil). They have no quality of eternal significance. Thus, the preacher points out that without theological underpinnings and vision, a person is unable "to find meaning in life unaided by divine revelation and interruption. This solo quest will always end in futility."[6]

The book of Ecclesiastes not only highlights the necessity of theologically examining the world around us but also provides us with the center of all theological thinking. Having examined the totality of humanity's pursuit and experience, the preacher concludes that meaning and purpose can only be found in fear of God and obedience to his commands. In other words, meaning and purpose in all life's endeavors are ultimately located in the pursuit of God. God is the starting point and ending point of all things. The character and activity of God and the obedience to his word are the central purpose of all humanity's existence. As Garrett summarizes, "The

6. Hamilton, "463 הָבַל."

insignificance of all done under the sun leaves him awestruck and silent before God. His inability to control or predict the future provokes him to dependence on God. The futility of attempting to secure his future through wisdom or acts of religion (e.g., making vows) leads him not to impiety but to an understanding of the true nature of obedient trust."[7]

The same is true of the church. Our perspective on ministry, our discovery of purpose and meaning, and the focus point of ministry begin and end with God. Connecting our theology to our ministry involves placing everything within the context of God's character and activity, as well as our relationship with him. When our understanding of God becomes the center of our theology and the bridge by which we engage, evaluate, and transform our local community, our efforts are joyous and strenuous activities in the art of ministry, even though portions of ministry remain enigmatic.[8]

Conclusion

After thirty-five years of pastoral ministry in rural communities, I again ask the question I asked years ago: "What does my eschatology have to say to a family in crisis?" The answer is everything! The promise of Christ's return to heal and restore a broken world gives us hope when the people we love face their brokenness. The church, struggling to exist in a dying community, discovers new life in the promise that God will build his church. A rancher who lost his crop in an unexpected hailstorm can find peace in the assurance that God will provide for his needs.

To be effective in rural ministry, we must not only understand how to bridge our theology to the lives of the people and churches we serve, but we must also view our ministry through the lens of our theology. We must see our theology as the foundation for ministry and the guide for our ministry.

This theological foundation is what we desire to accomplish in this book. In each chapter, leaders in rural ministry will guide us as we examine the struggles and challenges we face in ministry, placing these questions within the context of biblical theology and the ministry and people we serve in rural communities. When we establish a theology for our community, we can effectively navigate a changing and confusing world by contextualizing the gospel so that the people can relate. Furthermore, integrating our theology into our daily life and ministry provides hope to the pastor

7. Garrett, *Proverbs, Ecclesiastes, Song of Songs*, 345.

8. Kaiser, *Ecclesiastes*, 125.

and significance to the ministry. When we see our ministry through the lens of biblical theology, it changes our perspective. It reshapes our view of ministry by enabling us to see God's sovereign work in our lives and community. While the focus will be on the church's ministry within the rural community, we hope it will also provide a basis for theological reflection for all of life. Our theology answers the questions of why we perform our ministry (determining vision), what we do within our ministry (developing programs), where we serve in our ministry (discovering importance), and what outcome we desire to accomplish (defining success).

As we reflect on our theology and the churches we serve, we invite you, the reader, to engage in theological reflection and bridge your ministry in the rural church and community with the infinite being of God. Our desire in this book is to equip rural pastors to develop a theology for their ministry grounded in the word of God and shaped by his activity in the world. In the process, we will find that there is no insignificant ministry.

Part One

A Theological Perspective of Rural Communities

1

Is Rural Ministry a Priority for God?

John Adams

Why does rural ministry matter when large cities and global evangelism seem more strategic?

Most ministry efforts in North America and other nations aim at the population centers. Church-planting efforts focus on cities and suburbs. The largest churches in America grow in the most populated places. A certain amount of wisdom can be seen in bringing the gospel to the people who reside in concentrated areas. But like many good ideas, an unquestioned focus on cities has dramatically shifted ministry focus away from rural areas. Yet, one in six Americans are rural residents, some 46[1] to 60[2] million people. A strategy focused on population centers overlooks many who need Christ. If rural America were a nation, only twenty-four of the world's 234 countries would have a larger population.[3]

In addition to focusing on reaching people in population clusters, an urban-focused philosophy also aims to target people and places of cultural

1. Parker et al., "Demographic and Economic Trends," para 10.
2. America Counts, "What Is Rural America?"
3. Worldometer, "Countries in the World."

influence as a strategic way to reach a nation. It is possible, however, to lean so heavily on what seems strategic that we consider other methods or another focus to be in opposition to what we have deemed "strategic." City-primary logic suggests that impacting the largest concentration of people and reaching the culture shapers in influential cities is the way to evangelize America. Targeting cities with the good news of Christ will create an evangelistic ripple sweeping outward to the rest of the nation.

Yet, as part of a ministry serving churches in rural places since 1948 and personally serving in rural communities since 1995, scant evidence exists that gospel influence flowing outward from cities reaches rural communities. With few exceptions, the movement of pastors is away from rural places toward the cities. Occasionally, a city church will launch a church-planting effort in a rural location, or a multi-site church will plan a rural campus. However, these are rare compared to the number of pastors raised in rural places who move to minister in cities or suburbs.

While the logic of population density and influential people seems wise from a human perspective, perhaps that's not the only perspective Christ-followers should consider. Is it possible that our human wisdom about what is strategic conflicts with how God works? This chapter will examine the biblical record of God's nonstrategic work with Israel, the nonstrategic way he sent the Messiah, and the nonstrategic way he launched his church. City-primary thinkers have argued that the New Testament record of mission is primarily urban. Tim Keller expresses this view in *Why God Made Cities*:

> Look at the New Testament. Historical research shows that the early Christian missionaries in the Roman Empire did not go to the countryside. They did not go to small towns. Paul was the best example of this. They went into the cities and only the cities to preach the Gospel.[4]

Paul seems to focus primarily on cities, but he was not the only early Christian missionary. As we reexamine the overlooked portions of the New Testament record of the gospel mission, we will find that small towns and rural areas were a key focus of early evangelism. In addition, Paul's ministry launched missionaries who reached towns like Laodicea and Colossae, rural places where Paul did not personally preach. Additionally, we will find

4. Keller, *Why God Made Cities*, 29.

that the first missionaries who brought the message of Christ targeted rural areas and small towns.

Perhaps we have overlooked some theological values in rural ministry while prioritizing city ministry. Perhaps the biblical record reveals more than just the facts of God's work, displaying something of his character and attitude toward overlooked people.

God's Nonstrategic Work in Scripture

Reviewing God's work revealed through Scripture, we find his plan does not align with our definition of what might be strategic; in fact, it seems quite the opposite. Early in Genesis, God chooses Abram for reasons he only partially explains. Abram is the patriarch of one family, and while God does bless him and grant a measure of influence, his clan is not a regional power. Abram encounters influential kings, and as his family grows into a people group, they do so under the rule of the Egyptian nation. Only after their rescue from Egyptian bondage does God explain his choice of Israel's people. He declared in Deuteronomy:

> The Lord your God has chosen you to be a people for his treasured possession, out of all the peoples who are on the face of the earth. It was not because you were more in number than any other people that the Lord set his love on you and chose you, for you were the *fewest of all* peoples, but it is *because the Lord loves you* and is keeping the oath that he swore to your fathers, that the Lord has brought you out with a mighty hand and redeemed you from the house of slavery, from the hand of Pharaoh king of Egypt. Know therefore that the Lord your God is God, the faithful God who keeps covenant and steadfast love with those who love him and keep his commandments, to a thousand generations. (Deut 7:6–9 ESV; italics added)

God explains that his choice flows from his love, not their numerical size. "Israel" numbered just two when God called Abram and remained a small nation even at the height of their population. His love for them, not human strategic reasoning, prompted God to choose the people of Israel. God chose Israel as the object of his love and as his means of revealing his love to observing nations. Love, by its nature, is nonstrategic. Instead of seeking a self-enriching outcome, love seeks the best for the one loved. Love is individual, not something one can have for the masses. Because

God's love focuses on individuals, he doesn't require a threshold population size as an object of his love. God chose to love Abram and continued to love the people of Israel through the generations because of his covenant commitment to their forefathers.

Not only does God not need a large population, but he indicates that he chose Israel for their relative insignificance. His selection criteria preferred their relative unimportance by human standards. He chose a few over many, weak over strong, in choosing Israel. This intentional choice undercuts what humanity considers valuable: population size, military might, political allegiances, or territory held. When God inspired Deut 7, Israel still had none of those things. Apart from God's divine provision, they wouldn't have been able to escape Egypt and lacked the power to claim a homeland for themselves. God's lovingly sovereign choice appears in bright relief through Israel's lack of earthly value. Love chose them; human wisdom would have looked elsewhere.

Though it was not his will, God could have selected Egypt instead of Israel. They were one of the great regional powers in Abram's day. While it could seem more strategic and certainly would have impacted more lives, God chose tiny Israel over populous Egypt.

God's selection of Israel as his people seems to strip away what the world values to highlight God's love and the magnitude of his power. Almighty God chose insignificant people to receive his special revelation of truth. He chose them to experience his power and provision. He brought them into a relationship with him so they could represent him to the rest of the world from the margins rather than from the center of power. In choosing the people others considered less valuable, he opened the door for those who feel insignificant to come to him because he accepts even "lowly" Israel. In working with underpowered people, his unlimited power comes into clear focus.

God explains that this is not an accident of history; choosing the least of these is a feature of God's plan. He calls those who lack what the world values to show that worshipping him as God supplies a treasure more significant than the world can offer. We see the least-of-these dynamic at work when the Father sent the promised Messiah.

Messiah Sent to the Insignificant

From the Gospel accounts of Mary's conception and Christ's birth in Bethlehem, we see God disdains earthly ideas of importance. Joseph and Mary lack any form of status or wealth. Though both are of King David's lineage, they have no personal connection to wealth or power. They are the residents of a tiny and despised town in the boondocks of Israel. While Joseph was likely diligent in his work, his occupation was not influential.[5] Instead, Joseph worked with his back and hands rather than with his intellect and social relationships. He was a builder who constructed or repaired homes and implements for the village.[6] He may have traveled to nearby construction projects to work as skilled labor.

When Jesus was born, the Magi who heard of the birth expected a palace delivery, not an arrival in small-town Bethlehem. To add to the unexpected, this historic birth doesn't even occur in a dwelling. The angelic announcement spotlighted the nonstrategic nature of Christ's arrival, avoiding the religious and political leaders to appear to a small band of scruffy shepherds! Religious leaders disdained these semi-nomadic herdsmen for failing to prioritize observance of the sacred law and their periodic absence from the synagogue.[7] These men are hardly early cultural influencers. Due to the demands of their work and the odor of sheep, they were an isolated class of agricultural workers, yet God sent them not one angel but an entire choir! (Luke 2:8–20). God sent the long-awaited Messiah to a small town, a feed-trough cradle, and shepherds as first witnesses. Messiah's arrival turns human strategy on its head. His arrival was intentionally nonstrategic because Jesus's first mission was to the poor and marginalized. God prioritizes those who know they need his help; that's what love does.

Most of Jesus's earthly life was spent in obscurity, far from the influential center of Israel. Nazareth was just a town of under five hundred people[8] with a poor reputation (John 1:46). Dr. Clark notes, "While the brightest religious students were in Jerusalem studying the law, Jesus was in the remote, rural village of Nazareth learning carpentry."[9] Instead of building relationships with religious leaders or demonstrating his spiritual insights,

5. Koiter, "Nazareth."

6. Louw and Nida, s.v. "τέκτων." A builder in biblical times, one who was regarded as a tekton, would be skilled in the use of wood and stone and possibly even metal.

7. Maier, *In the Fullness of Time*, 44.

8. Koiter, "Nazareth."

9. Clark, "Rural Theology."

which he had presented at age twelve, Jesus remained in Galilee learning a manual trade. None of the people in his day would have seen the incredible significance of his young life.

When Jesus finally launched his earthly ministry, he chose to distance himself from the center of influence. Instead of populous Jerusalem, home to God's temple, the center of Jewish religious life, he launched his ministry eight miles outside Jericho.[10] After forty days in the wilderness, he turned away from Jerusalem and went north to rural Galilee. Jesus concentrated his ministry in the countryside, though about one-tenth of Israel's population lived in Jerusalem.[11] The lightly populated Galilee region was agriculturally fertile, producing a significant portion of Israel's grain, oil, wine, and fish.[12] The rural people who worked the land, raised animals, and fished the vast lake were the focus of most of Jesus's recorded ministry.

The Gospel accounts of Jesus's ministry employ various terms to describe the locations where people reside. The most common Greek word is *polis*, which often has the technical meaning of "population center," typically a walled city, such as Jerusalem. Yet, *polis* is also used in the Gospels non-technically, simply indicating a place where people live.[13] The vocabulary of the Gospels is more diverse when describing the small places, the towns and villages where Jesus ministered.

The Gospels record twenty-six occasions where Jesus went to small villages to minister or sent his disciples to such places. The majority of Jesus's recorded ministry is to rural people, more extensive than any other people group in the Gospels. He taught, did miracles, and trained disciples in rural places far more than in the large cities of Israel.[14]

The names of large cities in Israel other than Jerusalem and Jericho are surprisingly absent from the Gospels. Jesus is not mentioned entering Tiberias, Samaria, Sepphoris, or Scythopolis, though Scythopolis is named twice. Instead, as with the city of Caesarea Phillipi, when Jesus was near the city, we read that he ministered to villages around it, but we do not read that he entered it (Mark 8:27). Sepphoris is particularly notable since it is just four miles from Nazareth. As a builder, Joseph likely worked on an outdoor

10. Laney, *Baker's Concise Bible Atlas*, 200–201.

11. Christian History Institute, "Life & Times of Jesus of Nazareth."

12. Laney, "Galilee."

13. Nazareth, which is not a walled or large city (see Koiter, "Nazareth") is called *polis* in Matt 2:23 and Luke 2:4.

14. Clark, "Rural Theology."

auditorium built there in his lifetime. Yet, despite its proximity, we don't read of Jesus entering that city.

The Gospels record that Jesus spent very little time in Jerusalem, except for religious festivals, before the final week leading up to the crucifixion. Instead, his ministry occurs in the "towns and villages," plural, indicating too many to list by name. Three main Greek terms appear in the Gospels for small gatherings of dwellings that Jesus visited:

- *Kōmē*, a relatively unimportant population center or village, as in Mark 8:23, occurs twenty-six times in the Gospels.[15]
- *Chōra* is not a dwelling place but refers to land under cultivation or pasture. It occurs twenty-three times in the Gospels. But Mark 1:5 notes this as the area where people were coming from to hear John the Baptist, as well as from the city of Jerusalem. In John 4:35, Jesus says these "fields" (chora) are white for harvest, referring to residents of Sychar coming to hear him.[16]
- *Agros*, a small village, possibly as small as a collection of farms as found in Mark 6:56, occurs four times in the Gospels referring to dwelling places.[17]

By denoting the variety of rural locations, rather than bundling all of them under the general term for city, we see the Gospel writer's attentiveness to the rural background of Jesus's primary audience. Jesus took his message to the people of small towns and rural villages, much more than the cities. Even Capernaum, the Galilean hub for much of Jesus's ministry, though large for a village, had only about one thousand inhabitants.[18] This specificity in identifying the type of rural place contrasts starkly with the absence of any information about Jesus visiting the significant cities along his travel routes.

Though rural areas may seem nonstrategic to urban people, a significant rural-urban difference may lie behind Jesus's approach. Suppose one wished to bring an essential message to a large city like Jerusalem. In that case, one must identify a key person, a prominent location, or an effective communication method to reach the entire city. Jesus taught in the temple on several significant occasions and spoke with at least one of the ruling

15. Louw and Nida, s.v. "κώμη."
16. Louw and Nida, s.v. "χώρα."
17. Louw and Nida, s.v. "ἀγρός."
18. Crossan and Reed, *Excavating Jesus*, 83, 88.

members of the Sanhedrin, yet only a small fraction of the city responded to his message (John 3:1). Rural communities, however, operate under a different communication dynamic. Almost any resident may bring important news to the community. We observe this occurring in the village of Sychar in John 4. A woman who is an outcast in her village has enough voice to bring the entire town streaming out to meet a potential Messiah in response to her quizzical plea, "Can this be the Christ?" (John 4:29). The townspeople rush out to see and hear the rabbi, who has powerfully impacted their neighbor. This woman is the opposite of influential; she's notorious and ostracized, yet an entire village heard and responded to the message through her witness.

Ordinary Disciples

Jesus's choice of core disciples also reveals a preference for those from rural and Galilean backgrounds. These men were on the margins of Jewish culture, considered "uneducated, common men," with terms highlighting their lack of credentials and credibility in an urban context (Acts 4:13). From the perspective of Jerusalem at the time, these were entirely the wrong sort of disciples if one wished to launch an influential movement. Conversely, if one plans to connect with rural, salt-of-the-earth people, these disciples begin from a place of credibility. They understand rural life, speak with a Galilean accent, and most have the calloused hands earned by physical labor (Matt 26:73). These apostles seem ridiculous to the cultured religious and political elite, but Jesus individually selected them for his purposes.

When Jesus sent them out in pairs before the resurrection, he sent them to cities and villages as his heralds (Matt 10:11). Their role was to announce the kingdom of the Messiah everywhere, without overlooking even the smallest places. When Jesus commissioned his disciples after the resurrection, he sent them on a progressive mission. Empowered by his Holy Spirit, they would be his "witnesses in Jerusalem and in all Judea and Samaria, and to the end of the earth" (Acts 1:8). Since they were near Jerusalem, awaiting the Spirit's arrival, it is logical to begin in the city. As the events unfold, the presence of the Spirit results in fulfilled prophecy and powerful preaching in the same city where the Messiah was crucified fifty days earlier. Initially, many turn to Christ in faith, but Christ's Commission extends outward. They were to preach in Jerusalem but not to limit their witness to the city.

The Judean region around Jerusalem contained an array of villages and smaller gatherings of homes with rural Jews needing to hear the good news of their Messiah. Beyond them were gentile communities, with Samaria as a representative. This step in the progression of Christ's command required the first disciples to bridge barriers of culture and religion. Though Samaria was a name for a city, it is also a region, which is likely where Jesus sent them. Notice that the conclusion of Jesus's command does not say "and to the cities of the earth" but to *the end* of the earth. Jesus could have named significant cities at a great distance, such as Rome, or Alexandria in Egypt, or focused their attention on cities. Instead, he chose the furthest and least parts of the earth in this geographical progression, which, in double contrast to the nearby city of Jerusalem, would be distant and rural.

Theological Reflections on God's Methods

Our knowledge of God is limited to what he chooses to reveal. Our fallen intellect alone is insufficient, so we must exercise some humility in theology and ministry. We can and should use wisdom and planning in church planting and ministry leadership, but all our work must draw deeply on God's self-revelation. Methods the world finds effective *may* serve the church, but only after careful scrutiny in the light of God's word. Pragmatism alone may lead us to strategies that work by undermining God's purposes rather than accomplishing them.

So far in this chapter, we've traced God's choice of Israel rather than a world power. His choice to send Messiah to an nonstrategic couple for the opposite of a high-profile birth. Jesus chose to remain in obscurity for thirty years and then conduct his three-year ministry primarily in rural areas. His inner circle of disciples were predominantly rural people, and when Jesus sent them out, he included rural places as locations for them to preach. The Commission of Acts 1:8 specifically includes rural areas in Judea and has an end goal that is more rural than urban.

These choices made by Almighty God indicate that he defines *strategic* differently than humans. He chooses people who lack what our world values. Instead of selecting the plentiful and powerful, those with earthly reasons to seem significant, God invests effort in those who are marginalized. His strategy inverts what might seem like the most effective approach or the most strategic people in our minds. We know from other texts that God takes a particular interest in widows, orphans, and minority groups among his people (Deut 10:17–18; Ps 146:19; Jer 22:3). His self-giving love takes the spotlight by focusing on those who appear to have little to offer him in return. As part of his creation, what could anyone offer him that is not already his? Yet, God loves marginalized people, including the 17 percent of Americans living in rural communities today. Small and rural areas were ordinary in our nation just a century ago. Now that population centers have grown to have regional influence, a measure of stigma clings to rural residents, at least in the minds of the urban elite. Rural places and rural people certainly feel marginalized in many ways.

Change Comes from the Margins

History reveals that the marginalized are more open toward God and may become God's change agents. In every system, change comes from the margins, not the center. We see this in the technology world with fledgling Apple producing the innovative tech, not IBM, and the startup SpaceX rather than NASA innovating with rockets. Ralph Winter illustrates this principle in missions, showing that outsiders often brought the gospel to dominant cultures as slaves or refugees.[19] Only those not embroiled in the prevailing system can offer an alternative to what is widely accepted.

The first missionaries outside Israel were Jewish Christians being persecuted (Acts 8:4; 11:19–22). Ralph Winter points out that Christians on the margins of culture, slaves, and those considered criminals evangelized the Mediterranean empire of Rome. It wasn't the wealthy or powerful who unseated Roman paganism. Similarly, the Gothic tribes of northern Europe were also profoundly impacted by those on the cultural periphery. Christians expelled from Christianized Rome, including Arian heretics, began putting the Gothic language into writing and translating the Scriptures. The evangelization of the Viking empire primarily occurred through the capture and enslavement of Christian monks, with God again working from the margins.[20] God's marginalized agents of evangelism had a profound impact on each of these groups of people. Those who benefit from the dominant culture often fail to transform it, even when they embrace Jesus's mission. Instead, change most often comes from the margins: the outsiders and the oddballs.

This spiritual principle is illustrated in the Corinthian church, as Paul notes in his first letter to them:

19. Winter and Hawthorne, *Perspectives*, ch. 4.
20. Winter and Hawthorne, *Perspectives*, ch. 4.

> For consider your calling, brothers: not many of you were wise according to worldly standards, not many were powerful, not many were of noble birth. But God chose what is foolish in the world to shame the wise; God chose what is weak in the world to shame the strong; God chose what is low and despised in the world, even things that are not, to bring to nothing things that are. (1 Cor 1:26–28)

God intentionally called people to himself in opposition to the world's values. The text is not merely reporting that those lacking what the world values turned to Christ more readily. Paul argues that God *selected* non-strategic people. The Greek word for "chose" is also used for God's election of those saved. God intentionally and effectively called to faith those who lacked earthly influence, those from low social classes, and those who were less educated. God chose people from the margins of culture rather than the center to upend the dominant culture's values. This choice spotlights his power; he doesn't need people the world considers exceptional to accomplish extraordinary things. This passage teaches that God's method targets the world's value system for destruction. The Jewish people demanded supernatural signs, while the gentiles sought wisdom; however, both groups evaluated information based on their own values. God refuses to play by human rules when accomplishing his purpose. The evangelists who took the gospel to the Mediterranean were predominantly slaves or household servants.[21] These overlooked people were denied any formal influence in their culture. Yet their lives and quiet testimony positioned them as witnesses in many households. Within a few generations, the faith of slaves and servants had permeated the Roman Empire. God's choice seemed non-strategic, but it was highly effective for his mission.

Was Early Christianity Primarily Urban?

As noted earlier, a prevailing view today is that early Christians were primarily urban; however, this view overlooks critical elements of history. Thomas Robinson's publication of *Who Were the First Christians?* directly challenges the idea that the early church was exclusively urban. Robinson demonstrates that the popular estimate of six million Christians as an urban phenomenon in an empire of sixty million does not withstand examination. The empire's population was predominantly rural, with about 85

21. Kirchschlaeger, "Slavery and Early Christianity."

percent of its residents living in rural areas. If Christianity were exclusively urban, "Christians would have been overrunning the urban centers of the Roman Empire."[22] If, alternatively, Christians were a mere 10 percent of the urban population, this would "require a radical rethinking of the Christian presence . . . in the empire."[23] Robinson argues that a significant rural Christian presence more accurately reflects the historical reality. For the Christian population to have an equal number of urban and rural people, the cities would need to be 33 percent Christian, but the rural areas would only need to be 5.8 percent Christian. He concludes, "The weight of the evidence linking the urban and rural environments points to the likelihood of an early Christian presence in the countryside and a noticeable rustic complexion of the urban churches. If a rural and rustic element does not become a prominent factor in our reconstructions of early Christianity, we must revise almost every aspect of the urban portrait of the Christian movement."[24] Christianity penetrated the cities, but not without impacting the countryside where the empire's population resided.

What About Paul's Methods?

Some missiologists claim that Paul's exclusive practice was evangelism in large cities.[25] Paul's approach took him to cities, but not exclusively cities. The cities of the empire "were dots on a rural landscape."[26] As moderns, we can envision going from urban location to urban location without traversing a rural area, but travel in the ancient world was at a walking pace. The evangelists walked through the countryside to cities, encountering other travelers, agricultural workers, and rural residents. The evangelists depended on rural hospitality for journeys that were farther than a day's walk, since most public accommodations were disreputable. These overnight stays and shared meals would create natural opportunities for evangelism. We know that much of Paul's ministry travel was on foot, exposing him to the rural empire and likely offering frequent opportunities for evangelism.

Paul's methods focused on gathering places, and he often spoke in the synagogue first before preaching to gentiles. Paul sought locations where

22. Robinson, *Who Were*, 18.
23. Robinson, *Who Were*, 19.
24. Robinson, *Who Were*, 222.
25. Keller, *Why God Made Cities*, 29.
26. Robinson, *Who Were*, 96.

God-fearers gathered in communities without a synagogue, as in Acts 16. When people turned to Christ, they took the good news to nearby rural communities. We see evidence of this in the letter to the Colossian church. Colossae was an agricultural town overshadowed by two cities, Laodicea and Hierapolis, about a half-day journey from either city.[27] Historical records suggest that Paul had not visited Colossae, but the church was established due to his work in Laodicea (Col 4:15). Paul's letter to rural believers in Colossae reveals how he treasured them as family, though he hadn't personally met them. While Paul may have gone to cities to preach, he understood the gospel to include all people in all places. Both urban Ephesus and rural Colossae received heartfelt exhortations to grow in Christ and were each subject of Paul's earnest prayer. Paul's ministry had an urban center, but it also served as a launching point to reach the predominantly rural population.

Conclusion

The pattern of God's work recorded in Scripture shows he utilizes the weak and marginalized. He sent Messiah to the fringes of society to call those without cultural power to follow. The pattern of God's work suggests his strategy may appear nonstrategic to our eyes. His approach differs from what we might choose because his views and values differ from ours. Following Jesus's example, we must focus on the people and places at the margins rather than prioritizing population centers exclusively. God sent the Messiah to a people and a nation that was radically nonstrategic, yet the news of Christ's life, death, and resurrection has impacted billions of lives. His ragtag band of disciples brought the gospel to cities and villages around the Mediterranean in one generation.

The Acts 1:8 Commission includes both Jerusalem and rural Judea, so faithful efforts to fulfill our mission must prioritize city and rural outreach. While a ministry may specialize in reaching one type of community, we must be cautious not to denigrate other focus areas. Ministry in America and Western missions internationally have had a city-primary focus for decades. We are learning that this philosophy rests on a slanted view of early church history and selective reading of Scripture, so a renewed appreciation for rural ministry is in order. Since Jesus and his first disciples

27. Dunne, "Colossae."

concentrated their work in towns and villages, we imitate Christ as we serve among the people at the margins.

Implications

The pastor or missionary serving in a rural place or small town stands in the stream of God's work in this world. Ministry among people others overlook demonstrates that God cares for the few, the forgotten, and the marginalized. As Stephen Witmer notes, the committed and capable pastor serving in a small place is not present to gain prestige, wealth, or national influence.[28] Instead, they model the love of Christ for those others overlook. They are following in the footsteps of the Messiah, who invested his time in towns and villages. Their work is founded on the reality that God calls and uses ordinary people and that the true power to change lives resides not in the status or influence of the messenger but in the presence of God's Spirit.

Followers of Christ in rural places and small towns should take heart in God's work through history. He treasures those others disdain. He has repeatedly chosen the few and those considered insignificant to join his grand purpose. God routinely upends the world's values to accomplish his will. He sees people in rural places as so valuable that he sent his son to invite them into his kingdom. Those who join his work receive the power they need to do his will wherever he sends them.

Throughout the sweep of biblical history, marginalized people and rural areas are the objects of God's attention. Nothing in Scripture suggests that God has lost his love for rural people. Like the Jesus we follow, our world's towns, villages, and country areas need to hear the good news of Christ. They will need to listen to this message from someone who takes the time and effort to be present in small places and share the truth. As people turn to Christ, they need a shepherd to care for them, leading them toward maturity and compelling them to be a witness to their friends and neighbors in the community where God has planted them.

28. Witmer, *Big Gospel in Small Places*, 82.

2

Social Engagement with Spirit-Filled Rural Ministry

Rex J. Howe

My parents had already lived hard lives when they met. The difficulties they brought with them into the marriage continued to present challenges throughout their marriage. Even still, I experienced a safe, loving, and disciplined home life. I was sixteen years old when my parents divorced. I began drinking and living a promiscuous lifestyle of poor, confused, and angry decision-making. In the spring of 2001, a Christian friend invited me to an evangelistic event for college students at his local church. After two weeks of attendance, Christ became my Lord and Savior.

After many years of ministry and education, I returned to rural Appalachia. I now see many of the challenges my family and I faced were part of a much larger matrix of social issues. Substance abuse, divorce, poverty, fatherlessness, sexual immorality, local politics, and historical and cultural narratives in Appalachia all form part of the social context of the story. Within the full strength of these social storms, I experienced God's grace, which transformed my life.

The Significance of Rural Ministry in Social Issues

The rural church offered an alternative to these suffocating and peace-robbing realities, particularly in addressing personal, familial, and social issues. The people of Ohio Furnace Enterprise Baptist Church loved me as a boy. They communicated the gospel of Jesus Christ to my heart and mind. It is a truly Appalachian congregation with an anticipation of the Holy Spirit, testimony time in the worship service, three services a week, the washing of feet as an ordinance of the church, spontaneous singing and praise, and passionate, animated preaching from the pulpit. My favorite memories include congregational prayer time at the altar. The church building on the creek held seventy-five people in its sanctuary. The pastor served in a bivocational capacity. Amidst the many troubles I experienced as a youth, the volunteer youth leaders consistently showed me love and hope, encouraging me to trust in the gospel. This Appalachian church appears weak, out of the way, and powerless on a societal level. However, in such weakness, God grew the seeds they planted and watered in my life, from which came a power to overcome and to minister redemptively. The rural church offered an alternative reality: Christ and his word at the center of life, with the real presence and power of the Holy Spirit for living. The spiritual treasures in these small congregations challenged the common narratives and myths at the root of many of our social ills.

The Social Crises of Rural Communities

Race and Immigration in Rural Communities

When speaking about race and immigration, rural folks often carry ideas into contemporary conversations, which are helpful and harmful. Yet, the best of north central Appalachian Christianity brings deep insights into the grace of God lived in the white ghetto of Appalachia. Outsiders often mistake rural concepts of justice, order, and rightness as racism or hatred of immigrants rather than understanding they have a vision for mercy expressed through just and orderly governance for the sake of the well-being of all. Yet, Scripture provides rural Christians with a theological foundation for race-related issues. The rural Christian has been born again into God's forever family, which is a multi-racial community.

Poverty in Rural Communities

In the early 1900s, Portsmouth, Ohio, boomed.[1] Jobs were plentiful. Churches of every denomination were planted and thrived. The natural and seasonal beauties of the area rival the best in the world: the rivers, hills, and forests. It was a place to work, settle a family, and live all your days. Portsmouth industries included shoe, steel, atomic, railroad, and mercantile. After decades of success, the local employment base weakened, and industries declined. By 1980, all the major industries mentioned above either closed completely or experienced a significant decline. Unemployment soared, and the region became heavily dependent on government-based social welfare programs, a dependency that remains true for a large portion of the population today. The same story is repeated in rural communities across North America as the economy shifts to urban centers, leaving rural communities behind.

Drug Addiction, Trauma, and Recovery in Rural Communities

Following economic poverty and despair in southern Ohio, substance abuse raged during the surge of the pill mills of the 1990s and early 2000s as heroin dealers filled the vacuum left after law enforcement shut down corrupt pain clinics.

America's highest overdose death rate takes place in north central Appalachia.[2] Like many rural communities, substance abuse has shaken the foundations of the family, education, health care, economy, religion, and politics. When stripped of biblical spirituality, social and medical studies fail to show what is behind all the trauma and inner human inclinations toward substance abuse. Biblical and theological foundations can equip the rural church to minister effectively in the social darkness of childhood trauma and substance abuse. The rural church possesses resources for people impacted by trauma, struggling with excess, and caught in abusive living.[3]

1. Byrne et al., *Thirst for Land.*
2. Ohio Department of Health, *Preliminary Data Summary.*
3. For further information see Clements, *Trauma Informed Church.*

Mental Health Stigma in Rural Communities

Once spiritual foundational truths are established, people need resources to grow, mature, and flourish. These resources are often lacking in rural communities. An additional problem surfaces when resources are available but underutilized. The stigma about mental health in rural communities is real. An equipped rural church offers people biblical solutions to life's problems without the stigma found in going to a mental health professional.

Outward Migration of Young People in Rural Communities

Many rural people remain in their home communities; however, the outward migration of young people for education and employment is well-known in rural places. The realities of migration are not reflected in the same way in every rural community. Yet, clear evidence of an aging population, due to the migration of younger people from the area, can be consistently seen in rural areas. Migration often results from a lack of local opportunities in employment, education, entertainment, and other personal and professional developmental resources. Consequently, many rural churches struggle to cultivate a missional perspective about "home" that addresses outward migration.

Broken Families in Rural Communities

The cycle of addiction, trauma, and broken families describes the kind of whirlwind in which many rural families find themselves. I'll never forget the road trip conversation with my children about my own extended family. They asked, "Daddy, is *everyone* in your family divorced?" At first, I hesitated to answer as I surveyed each couple in the extended family. Finally, I admitted to them, "Yes, it is sad to say that is true." I encouraged them with the strength of my resolve to never divorce their mother and guided them that we should pray for God to continue to redeem our family by strengthening what marriages now exist by his grace. Their mother and I often explain that broken families are a significant reason we returned to Appalachia and dedicated ourselves to children's ministry in our local church.

Politics in Rural Communities

Rural people think deeply about international matters, have strong opinions, and carefully weigh the spiritual realities behind international politics: evil, good, justice, mercy, demonic interference, and the mission of God. Like many Americans, rural people are well-acquainted with the sharp division in national and state-level politics. Until recently, families typically shared generational solidarity in their political heritage and party commitment. That has changed. As national parties have divided themselves into moderate and extreme entities, it has changed the political conversations at rural family gatherings. While significant shifts in national culture tend to stir up the most emotion and conversation, the governance of state and local political leaders provides access to resources that enable rural people to thrive where they are.

Local politics play a significant role in the day-to-day life of the rural person: school boards, mayors, township trustees, the local sheriff, and local issues decided by voters. Relationships and networking can become a space that tempts even good people to abuse power and give in to greed. At the same time, it's challenging to lead in a small town where everyone knows you and has expectations because of that knowledge, which can affect one's ability to govern impartially.

Biblical Foundations of Social Engagement in the New Testament Communities

The Spirit-filled local church is the greatest resource in a rural community. It provides a community for common belonging, finding wholeness, learning stewardship, serving in mission, and growing in a common confession of faith. The variety of gifts, talents, and professions is unmatched by other organizations—teachers, medical professionals, folks with financial expertise, craftsmen and women, landowners, merciful caregivers, and multigenerational wisdom for the trials of life. To these elements, add the presence, wisdom, and power of the Holy Spirit. The rural church gains its way of life from the Bible.

Biblical Belonging: Matters of Marginalization, Race, and Family

The New Testament church is a temple, unlike the ancient temples in Jerusalem. Peter called Christians "living stones," who were being built up into a "spiritual house" (1 Pet 2:4–6). After his well-known teaching on salvation by grace through faith in Eph 2:1–10, Paul continued to explain how this grace has brought the once marginalized gentiles near to the promises of God in Christ. He painted the picture of Jews and gentiles in Christ built up together into a temple, sharing the same foundation—Christ the cornerstone and the apostles and prophets—and indwelt by the same Holy Spirit. The temple imagery in Peter's and Paul's writings offers a vision of how formerly marginalized and divided groups of people become one entity, belonging and sharing in God's grace in Christ. As a *decentralized* temple, the disciples of Jesus Christ are called to make disciples of all nations. He bestowed the Holy Spirit on his church so that we would be his witnesses locally, nationally, and internationally.

From its founding at Pentecost, the church of Jesus Christ is a growing, diverse, and unified family (Acts 2, 11, 13, 15). Since the beginning, Christians have referred to one another as brothers and sisters (e.g., Acts 15:23, 40). The internal maturity of its members looks to elder brothers and sisters for the guidance of the younger (e.g., 1 Tim 5; Titus 2). Having the same Spirit dwelling in us who raised Jesus from the dead (Rom 8), we cry out with one voice to the same Father, "Abba!" When the Lord taught his disciples to pray, he didn't start with "My Father" but "Our Father" (Matt 6:9). We are one family, with one God, one Lord, one Spirit, one faith, one baptism, and one hope (Eph 4). Remember what Jesus said in the Gospel of Mark when he was told that his mother and brothers had come to seize him? They thought that he was out of his mind. He asks the crowd, "Who are my mother and brothers?" Looking at the crowd, he answered, "Whoever does the will of God, he is my brother and sister and mother" (Mark 3:31–35). In the church, we have one Father, and we have innumerable family members.

The biblical concepts of temple and family provide belonging for people who have experienced the trauma of racism or the crisis and pain of a broken home. These biblical principles empower redemptive living in the troubles encountered by rural families. The rural church offers a sense of belonging to individuals marginalized by limitations beyond their control.

Biblical Wholeness: Matters of Spirit, Soul, and Body

In a broken world where sin has affected every facet of the human identity, the Bible offers redemption to the whole human. For rural people who have experienced trauma, addiction, broken homes, depression, anxiety, and other kinds of serious trouble, the church family not only provides a place to belong but also provides a personal, inner, and spiritual renewal of mind and heart to experience through Christ by the Holy Spirit. Galatians 5:16–24 offers an example of the transformation that occurs in a person by the Holy Spirit (see also Eph 4:25–32). The Holy Spirit opposes the sinful nature of humanity, which is the true root of every social problem that has ever existed in every human community.

In evangelistic conversations, people describe "what's wrong with the world" as greed, abuse of power, violence, lack of education, or failure to distribute resources to the people most in need. While I agree that all these things are related to our problems, they are not the *root cause* of societal ills. The human condition, specifically the sinful nature (e.g., Matt 15:10–20; Rom 3:10–18; note the Old Testament references in the Romans passage), is the root problem that gives timeless explanatory power to social issues. If we merely work on treating the traumatized without asking why humans traumatize each other, we fail to transform the situation.

The church stewards a gospel that is "the power of God for salvation" (Rom 1:16) for the whole human person. Rural Christian pastors, counselors, and church members can enter complicated conversations with a unique hope and transformative power. People, families, and communities are not left entirely and only to the snares and schemes of sin, whether we think of sin in personal, communal, historic, or cosmic terms.

Biblical Stewardship: Matters of Leadership and Resources

The Bible gives a precise aim for what God expects of the people with whom he has entrusted his gospel, his Spirit, and his word: "This is how one should regard us, as servants of Christ and stewards of the mysteries of God. Moreover, it is required of stewards that they be found faithful" (1 Cor 4:1–2 ESV). Stewardship is a sacred calling to carry out the mission that you have received faithfully. Jesus told us what leadership among his followers should look like in Mark 10:42–45. Leaders are servants. They are called to faithfully steward what God has entrusted to them to serve all people, especially the household of faith, for the Great Commission of Jesus Christ to make disciples. Peter writes, "As each has received a gift, use it to serve one another, as good stewards of God's varied grace: whoever speaks, as one who speaks oracles of God; whoever serves, as one who serves by the strength that God supplies—so that in everything God may be glorified through Jesus Christ" (1 Pet 4:10–11 ESV). The Holy Spirit sovereignly distributes his gifts for Christ's Commission through the church. It has always been true in the story of God's people that his power and presence in them can strengthen the surrounding communities, cities, and countries in which they live by both the good that they work and by the confrontation of evil and wickedness.

Biblical Mission: Matters of Migration, Youth, Mission, and Politics

In Acts, the Holy Spirit set apart men and women to be Christ's witnesses locally, regionally, nationally, and internationally. We follow the missionary journeys of Peter, Barnabas, Apollos, and especially Paul (Acts 1:8; 13:1–3). The approach of the latter fulfilled the Commission of Christ by completing three short-term trips, each ending with a field report back home. Imagine three layers to developing a missional mindset in a rural church: (1) prepare them for God's call to "home" as a legitimate mission field, (2) prepare them for God's call to short-term excursions away from "home base" to the needy mission fields in other parts of the county, state, nation, or world, and (3) prepare them for God's call to more permanent migrations away from "home" for the glory of God and the mission of Christ. Our young people who have believed in Christ are now commissioned in the great mission. The Holy Spirit indwells them and gives them the mind of Christ. This is our spiritual reality as the people of God; hand-wringing about migration betrays a lack of missional clarity and spiritual discernment.

God has sovereignly appointed our stays, migrations, and returns (Acts 17:26–27). To make the kind of social impact that will transform, rural churches must return to Christ's Commission as the central focus of our activity and discipleship. Only when the mission of discipleship and our longing for Christ are central will our people maximize their impact on regional economics, education, entertainment, and personal and professional development; this begins with local leaders becoming models for ministry and leadership.

Many rural men are often resistant to serving in local church leadership, and as a result, they fail to lead transformation *from* the church *into* the surrounding community. They feel ill-equipped to serve in local church leadership. Local churches need a plan for training leaders to equip them with the knowledge, skills, and vision necessary to transform their community through the local church's mission.

Many young people do not grow up with a vision for local church ministry and leadership (whether vocational or non-vocational) because it is not modeled for them. They see an important, yet limited, leadership exhibited when believers devote all their resources outside the local church. For young people to fulfill their ministries, they need to receive a model and vision for spiritual and servant leadership within the local church. An opportunity exists for the local rural church to be the exemplary model of godly, Spirit-filled leadership in their communities, preparing young people for the life God has called them to. Many of our greatest people resources are being expended at the local firehouse or school board. It's not that this participation should stop; instead, it needs to originate from the rural church, equipping its leaders with a mindset for the mission.

Biblical Confession: Matters of Love and Loyalty

The purest love and loyalty ever to be manifested exists within the Trinity. The Father, the Son, and the Holy Spirit share a pure and perfect love. The loyalty within the Trinity is also unmatched. Therefore, the church that confesses the faith of the triune God and that experiences the presence of the Holy Spirit should be marked by this purest of love and loyalty in its horizontal relationship with other humans. While many relational issues exist in local churches that hinder their witness in the broader community and, therefore, limit their ability to impact social needs, no rural relationship matter needs to be addressed more than Christian marriages.

Traditional, rural communities have not remained untouched by divorce. While some reason that divorce rates reflect a positive empowerment of women[4] in rural communities, they fail to acknowledge the wreckage in the lives of the children of divorce.[5] Rural churches can strengthen and support marriages, especially for impoverished couples and those facing the parenting challenges of middle age. There are two levels to this: (1)

4. Tavernise and Gebeloff, "Once Rare."

5. Root, *Children of Divorce.*

identify the biblical and theological truths that should serve as foundational for marriage (i.e., the Trinity, the ministries of the Holy Spirit, etc.), and (2) integrate these truths into the teachings, ministries, and relationships that you build into married people's spiritual lives.

While a church can do many things to support and strengthen marriages, lack of commitment and infidelity are at the top of the list of causes that bring marriages to an end. These are theological and spiritual issues at their root. For too long, the church has failed to disciple in a way that strengthens marriages in the love and loyalty of the Spirit of the triune God whom we confess. Divorce shakes the foundations of rural communities, changing the landscapes of homes, churches, schools, public service, and all other relational networks. The theological foundations on which the Scriptures say Christian marriage rests are the love and loyalty of the triune, creator God, who demonstrated his love for us in that while we were still sinners, Christ died for us (Rom 5:8).

Theological Foundations in Pneumatology for Social Engagement

The Failure of the Social Gospel in Rural Contexts

Our communities often depend upon the governmental, social, and even religious responses to the social issues raised in this chapter. However, governmental, activist, or religious "liberators" claiming to have an outsider solution that promises to transform rural communities into resembling "enlightened" urban and suburban communities often misunderstand and miscalculate the values and preexisting resources of rural people.

Grounding Social Action in Our Theology of the Holy Spirit

The Essentiality of the Spirit in Rural Ministry

As water, fire, wind, and breath are essential to creation, so is the Holy Spirit for life and ministry. Thankfully, God's revelation in Scripture has given us more than vocabulary words and imagery. The Bible records the teachings of the prophets, the apostles, and Jesus Christ on the Holy Spirit. Larry Hurtado described the Holy Spirit as essential to the New Testament's discourse about God.[6] That is to say, one cannot discuss the God of the New Testament without discussing the early Christian experience and testimony about the Holy Spirit.

The rural church needs the Holy Spirit; it is a *spiritual* people. Reasoning our way out of dependence on the Spirit for life and ministry is dangerous.[7] The Spirit-illuminated and -filled church transformed a city like Ephesus in Paul's day (Acts 19). The power of the Spirit through the preaching of the gospel from the Scriptures caused people to turn from dark magic, abandon idolatry, reject sexual immorality associated with their old religion, irritate the greedy, impact politics, transform households, overcome racism, generate a community of sharing that met physical needs, and set free a missionary movement that reached an entire region in a relatively short amount of time.

The Exposition of the Spirit for Rural Ministry

Greg Heisler wrote in his book *Spirit-Led Preaching*,

> The underlying foundation of the spirit-led definition [of expository preaching] assumes we can see the Holy Bible and the Holy Spirit as complementary to each other instead of competing against each other. Spirit-led preaching seeks to overcome the false dichotomy between the Word and the Spirit and instead unites them as the powerful catalyst for Spirit-demonstrated preaching.[8]

Heisler instructs that expository preaching is driven by the Holy Spirit along the path of the text (like train tracks) with the final destination not merely of proper exegesis or preaching methodology but of christological witness and Spirit-led obedience.

The rural church needs Spirit-illuminated preaching and listening so that the saints are equipped to do the work of the ministry. It is under the preaching of the word that both the shepherd and the flock learn the truth and learn to love in a way that brings life, wisdom, and righteousness into their social circles. This ministry of Scripture and Spirit means that the rural church possesses the resources that have always been essential for transformation.

6. Hurtado, *God in New Testament Theology*, 73–94.
7. Sawyer and Wallace, *Who's Afraid of the Holy Spirit?*
8. Heisler, *Spirit-Led Preaching*, 21.

The Experience of the Spirit in Rural Ministry

The internal witness of the Holy Spirit assures the believer of salvation, adoption, sanctification, and forgiveness of sins (see Rom 8:16; Heb 10:4–18). The Spirit of Christ—who breathed out Scripture through the prophets, illuminated their inquiries, anointed the Savior for life, death, and resurrection, and announced this gospel through the apostles—is the same Spirit who now indwells believers (1 Pet 1:10–12). The remarkable reality of the Scripture-breathing Spirit indwelling the rural church to illuminate the Scripture for life and ministry is an experience that should be sought. The experience of Scripture and Spirit equips us with hope for Jesus's return and obedience in the world (v. 13). The Holy Spirit also brings into the church a future-oriented hope and perseverance (see Rom 8:26–29; Eph 1:13–14). In the presence of this Spirit, the church should put up its sails!

As the rural church navigates complex social issues, the Holy Spirit also helps the church distinguish truth from error. First John 4:1–6 presents a key passage for spiritual discernment in the local church. Rural churches test the spirits by the apostolic confessions concerning Jesus Christ. The content of the confessions includes: Jesus Christ has come in the flesh (1 John 4:2), is the Son of God (Matt 16:16–17; 1 John 4:15), and is Lord (Rom 10:9–10). The church participates by testing every prophecy (1 Thess 5:21).

The church that holds fast to the christological confession demonstrates a certain quality of love. God is love (1 John 4:16). We know love by God's sending of the Son into the world to make propitiation (1 John 3:16). The Spirit of truth in the church imitates Christ's self-giving love (1 John 3:16–18). The NET Bible study note on 1 John 4:2 comments, "Since the Holy Spirit is not the only Spirit active in the world, the author needs to qualify for the recipients how to tell if a spirit comes from God. The 'test' is the confession in 4:2." We test all teachings by this confession and all living by this confession.

As people from the community are evangelized, believe, receive instruction, confess Christ publicly, join the church, and sit at the Lord's Table, rural churches should approach discipleship expecting to experience the christological confession in the doctrine and ways of living of new members. However, for new members who once lived in the world regarding marriage, parenting, finances, substance abuse, racism, sexuality, politics, and poverty, the new christological confession that now lives in them by the Spirit transforms their way of living (see 2 Cor 5:17–20).

Ministry Implications for the Rural Church in Social Problems Through Pneumatology

The Church as Spiritual Symbol in the Rural Community

The Spirit resides in the rural church, making it a spiritual symbol in the community. A symbol is a tangible object that represents or extends to something unseen. The Spirit-filled church helps people around them imagine an alternative reality to the world as they know it. The existence of a rural church in a community is a constant invitation to its neighbors to reimagine life God's way with God's help.

The Church's Spiritual Function in the Rural Community

The Holy Spirit energizes the operations and activities of the church in a rural community. In settings where the historic social gospel has taken hold as the means for liberation from social ills, the church has abandoned its spiritual substance and life for the strategies of government and activism. When this happens, the church dies or becomes a shell with no substance. The rural church, where the Spirit dwells, always bears the biblical christological confession and love consistent with this confession. It does not abandon the word of God because it is the Spirit's word. It gives time, talents, and treasures because the same Spirit who remained with Jesus on the cross and in the resurrection now resides in the church. The Spirit creates belonging and unity around the christological confession of the church, which transcends all kinds of impenetrable social segregations seen in the world. In this sense, the church's function in a rural community is still prophetic and apostolic. It is not uttering a new revelation, but it is the one entity that continues to interpret and proclaim the existing revelation in the Bible. The church is also a "sent" people; we are missionaries making disciples.

The Church in Spiritual Conflict in the Rural Community

The rural church also presents a spiritual conflict in the community in which it resides. The Spirit in the church produces a particular evaluation of the history of the world, an assessment of the way of the world in the present, and the hope of a new creation in the future. The Spirit-filled church possesses a worldview that often conflicts with that of governments, schools, modern medicine, philosophies, activists, funeral homes, local businesses, youth sports leagues, and even households. Jesus said, "Do not think that I have come to bring peace to the earth. I have not come to bring peace, but a sword" (Matt 10:34). While God has positioned the church to bring blessing to the community in which it resides, Christ bestows his Spirit upon the church to be a beacon of light in the darkness.

Conclusion

The chapter began with a presentation of numerous social problems in rural contexts, with a particular focus on rural Appalachia.[9] A survey of the New Testament revealed that early Christians also faced social issues, which laid the groundwork for us to consider a theological concept that contemporary, rural Christians share with our earliest brothers and sisters. Pneumatology has emerged as a common theological foundation that has historically empowered the church to have a social impact. While the Spirit is mysterious and elusive,[10] he is also revealed and essential to the life and experience of the church. The chapter showed the Spirit-led exposition of Scripture as one of the significant contributions of the rural church to the community in which it resides. The section on pneumatology calls for the rural church to return to spiritual living and to experience the biblical presence of the Holy Spirit. Finally, rural ministry implications were briefly considered. The rural church, as a spiritual symbol, invites its community to envision an alternative to the world's ways. The church presents a tangible people and place that extends to a better reality. The spiritual function of the church in society has been described by many as a spiritual immune system; however, to fulfill this role, the rural church cannot abandon its Scripture- and Spirit-oriented ministries. The rural church also exists to create spiritual conflict. The New Testament reveals the realities of spiritual warfare and promises that the church will overcome. The rural church must stand its ground on truth and love well, matching the christological confession of the Spirit within it.

9. For an important resource on Appalachian pneumatology, see Schermerhorn and Mills, *Correct View*.

10. Ramm, *Rapping About the Spirit*, 7.

3

Let Your Light Shine

The Rural Church as a Change Agent

Jon Hansen

Effective ministry involves being a moral and spiritual change agent. Changing the community begins by presenting the indwelling Christ in you to the people who do not have the indwelling Christ in them, so that real change can take place. The Lord calls us to be salt and light (Matt 5:16). Just as light transforms darkness and salt purifies, so a spiritually vital church will affect its community.

Being salt and light in a community goes to the heart of God's redemptive plan. God calls the church to be involved in a ministry of change that engages people in the community who are not saved and are dealing with sin's consequences in their own lives. God's redemptive program, which includes justification, sanctification, and ultimately glorification, starts with Christ's redemptive work and the work of the Holy Spirit in people's lives.

God's plan includes using us to take the gospel to the lost world while sanctifying us. In Eph 2:1–10, Paul highlights that God intends to use our transformed lives as a testimony to the world that he is the ultimate agent of change. When the world sees the change God is making in us by how we live, they will wonder why, and then we can share Christ with them (1 Pet 3:15). We are told in Acts 1:8 that we are to be the Lord's witnesses in all the world. Christ left us here to be sanctified so that we are ready for heaven, but he also left us here to meet the physical and spiritual needs of others to demonstrate that God cares and loves all people. Jesus demonstrated compassion for people in his earthly life by meeting their temporal needs, so that they would accept his plan for addressing their most significant need of all—reconciliation with God, also known as eternal life. Second Corinthians 5:18–20 tells us that we have been given this ministry of reconciliation. We are involved in our communities to manifest Christ and demonstrate to the world that they are loved by God, who wants to meet their needs and have a personal relationship with them. If we say we represent Jesus, we should live like him, demonstrating the same care and compassion he had for the people he encountered. The church in the community is to be Christ-centered, which involves being others-centered. We minister because we are Christ's representatives to the world, including the community.

To change a community, God starts by changing and indwelling the individual. This individual is put into a community of other God-indwelt people—the local church. The church and pastor need to be in sync to impact the community through the indwelling of Christ. God is the ultimate change agent, as we see in John 3:16.

God saw that the people he created needed to be redeemed and changed, so he started an amazing chain of events. He loved us, saw our need, and sent his Son to be the ultimate change agent. He gathered a group of people (his disciples) and led them to change personally. Then, he sent them out to be change agents who led others to become change agents. In this way, the church was formed. But the process did not end there. People within those churches were to be change agents at home, in their neighborhoods, at work, and even beyond. The apostle Paul modeled this same method. He would go to a place, lead people to Christ, form a church, help that church select a pastor, and urge that pastor and church to impact their community.

The New Testament makes it clear that Jesus came to change lives, and after the indwelling of the Holy Spirit changes us, we become Christ's representatives of change to the world. Galatians 2:20 says that at salvation, we are changed. From that point, Christ lives his life in us. Theologian Major Ian Thomas expressed this in his book *The Saving Life of Christ*: "We have begun to see that Christian living is not a method or technique; it is an entirely different, revolutionary principle of life. It is the principle of an exchanged life—not I, but Christ liveth in me (Gal 2:20b)."[1] Earlier in the book, he wrote, "The One who calls you to go into all the world and preach the Gospel to every creature is the One who, by your consent, goes into all the world and preaches the Gospel to every creature through you!"[2]

How should the church today follow this biblical model? I encourage you to think of each community in rural North America as a circle. In his book *A Big Gospel in Small Places*, Stephen Witmer says, "Community matters to those who live within the circle of a small town. It should matter to small-town churches, too. We should aim to be local churches."[3] When God wants to impact a community positively, he begins by changing us first. Then, he puts us into a community of transformed people (the church). Then, the church reaches out to impact its community (what I call "the circle"). God sends the pastor into the community to connect with other change agents (the rest of the church) and positively impact the community for Christ. As the pastor and the church begin to affect their community as change agents, more people see and experience God's power to transform lives. We are called to be change agents just like Christ and to proclaim the same message he did: the message of the gospel.

A typical scenario might involve a Christ-indwelled pastor joining the circle of a rural community. He is ready to go to work reaching the community with the gospel, but he faces a significant obstacle: the church itself is unhealthy and has lost its focus on the gospel. He is tempted to bypass the church and be a Lone Ranger change agent.

That is not God's model. Until the pastor and the local church are in sync, they will fail to have a lasting gospel-centered effect on the community. God calls the pastor to work in concert with other Christ-followers, who are part of the local church. God never intended us to work alone; he designed us to function as a gospel-centered community (the church) to impact the greater community.

How does the gospel-centered pastor sync with the local church to form an effective gospel-centered team? To reach people with the gospel, Christ and Paul did not remain separate from the people they sought to reach. Instead, they sought to integrate themselves into the community. An effective change agent collaborates closely with the local church to have a positive impact on the community. This involves seven critical steps to

1. Thomas, *Saving Life Of Christ*, 23.
2. Thomas, *Saving Life of Christ*, 15.
3. Witmer, *Big Gospel in Small Places*, 116.

synchronize the ministry of the pastor and the local church, enabling them to work together rather than against each other in transforming their community. Both Jesus and Paul modeled these principles.

1. Explore and Evaluate

Working together starts with the new pastor and the church getting to know each other. At the same time, the pastor begins to explore the community. The goal is to evaluate the state of the church, its needs, and those of the community. Jesus and Paul both started their ministries by assessing the need. In many cases where well-intended ministry falls apart, the church and leadership have not taken the time to know each other or the people they are called to reach. The team must know the Lord and each other first and then together seek to know and understand the people they wish to impact.

The exploration and evaluation process may seem slow, but it is essential and foundational for effective ministry in the future. We need to resist the temptation to make changes immediately; instead, we must take the time to gain a deep, accurate understanding, thereby developing a ministry that connects with the people we serve. Remember the men of Issachar in 1 Chr 12:32, who understood the times and what God wanted them to do.

When I started ministry as a missionary pastor with a new church, I was given two pieces of advice that proved invaluable. First, remember that effective ministry is often a long, slow process. Second, remember that this is ultimately God's work, which he achieves through us, rather than our ministry for him. In Phil 1:6, Paul reminds us to trust God and his timing: "He who began a good work in you will carry it on to completion until the day of Christ Jesus" (NIV).

After years of ministry, I would add a third piece of advice to new pastors: Remember that the church is the body, and Christ is the head (see 1 Cor 12). Therefore, as the body, the pastor and the church must work together. It is essential to take the time to get to know each other. To effectively lead the church, we need to understand the people we serve. We first need to be a student of the church. Before the pastor can effectively lead the church, he needs to:

Study the history of the church he is serving in.

Study the church's doctrine.

Study the church's practices.

Study the lifestyles of the people of the church.

Study people's needs.

These principles can also be applied to the community we want to impact. Likewise, he needs to:

Study the historical and economic background of the community.

Study the events that had a positive or negative impact on the community.

Study the beliefs of the community.

Study its religious and ethnic background.

Study the community's practices.

Study the lifestyles of the people.

Study the needs of the community.

2. Educate

Once the pastor and church understand the culture and needs of the community, the church needs to be *educated* in what the Lord says they should know to be a genuinely gospel-centered church ready to do ministry.

In 2 Tim 4:1–5, Paul identifies the curriculum we should use: the word of God.

Jesus and Paul educated those they were encouraging to be change agents, and we need to do the same. If God's people do not know God's word, they will not know how to live and will have nothing of value to share with those who need to experience the change that comes from knowing Christ.

Acts 2:41–47 demonstrates that knowledge of the word of God is vital for the change-agent church to be healthy and ready to receive new believers. For the church to have a genuinely gospel-centered, culture-impacting ministry, its leaders must preach and live by the word. The church cannot hope to change its community without allowing God's word to dwell in and change its members. This indwelling only comes by education through study and application (Col 3:16–17 and 2 Tim 2:15). This process of education involves:

Preaching and teaching the word in the language of the people.

Preaching and teaching the word on the level of the people.

Loving people and building relationships with the people.

Modeling what you are teaching.

Coaching people to apply what you have been teaching and preaching.

Being patient with people as they learn.

Discipling leaders from among the people.

3. Empower for Ministry

When developing change agents in the local rural church to impact the community, the goal is to empower them to carry out the ministry intentionally. Jesus and Paul trained their followers and empowered them to continue the ministry. Jesus and Paul gave their followers the freedom to fail or succeed independently. Look again at Matt 28:18–20 and 2 Tim 2:1–2. Christian leaders are commissioned to hand over the work to others who are prepared to be change agents. According to Acts 2:43–44, a healthy change-agent church will be known for working together in the ministry. In Acts 2:44–45, the church is filled with change agents working together in ministry, not just the pastor doing all the work. Romans 12:3–8 explains why stepping back and allowing fellow change agents to minister themselves is essential.

Pastors should encourage fellow change agents to utilize their spiritual gifts within the church, enabling them also to apply these gifts in the community. An influential change-agent church will be one where people experience ministry, are free to learn from those in leadership how to do ministry, and even question leadership freely.

4. Foster an Environment of Mentoring

A healthy church is essential for being a mentoring church. Acts 2:42–47 describes a spiritually vital or healthy church ready to prepare or mentor its people for ministry. The local church was known for "praising God and having favor with all the people. And the Lord was adding to their number daily those who were being saved" (v. 47).

When examining the church in Acts, note that when the local church is healthy, exhibiting the four vital signs of Bible teaching, fellowship, prayer, and worship, God honors the fifth sign of evangelism by adding newly changed people from the community to the church. These new believers are ready to be mentored (discipled) by the healthy church and to become change agents.

5. Encourage

When a church of change agents is healthy, they enjoy being together, studying, praying, worshiping, and fellowshipping. They are ready to engage their community and represent Jesus by serving people in his name. In Heb 10, we are told that because of our salvation in Christ, we are to encourage one another to love and do good works in anticipation of Christ's return. Romans 12 says that the reason we conform to Christ is as a spiritual act of worship. We live out the Christian life in the community because Christ wishes to glorify the Father by using changed lives.

The Scripture gives us a clear picture of what a changed life looks like. James states that "pure" religion is taking care of people who can't take care of themselves, the dispossessed, and the voiceless, like widows and orphans (Jas 1:27). Micah likewise states that God requires that we seek justice, show mercy, and live humbly with God (Mic 6:8).

Because we are the body of Christ in the world, we sacrifice to help others. We allow him to minister through us. He is the fundamental change agent. We are just the instrument that he uses to impact the community. Because he lived a life of love, we are to live a life of love. Because he lived a life of sacrifice, we are to live a life of sacrifice. Because he ministered to people's needs, we are to minister to people's needs. Because he was a change agent, we are called to be change agents as well.

In Phil 2:1–18, we are told to be imitators of Christ. We are to think like him. We do ministry out in the community because he did, and now, he wants to continue his ministry through us. James 1 says we must be both hearers and doers of the word. Rev. T. DeWitt Talmage said, "I like the Bible folded between lids of cloth, or calfskin, or morocco, but I like it better when, in the shape of a man, it goes out into the world—a Bible illustrated."[4] We are to be the Bible illustrated in our communities. We are to take the message God gave us and live it out before the world.

4. Talmage, *Pathway of Life*, 278.

6. Engage in Planning for and Carrying Out the Ministry of Change

Matthew 5:1–16 gives us principles for effectively impacting our communities for Christ. In verses 1–2, we observe that Jesus planned for ministry. The church must do the same.

Verses 3–16 describe nine character qualities that a church should be known for in the community. We should be known as those who let Christ live and work through us, as evidenced by the fruits of the Spirit (Gal 5:22). When Matt 5 is compared to Gal 5:22, a Christian can see what they are called to:

1. Live as poor people (v. 3) who exhibit true love to others by sharing what we have, including the truth.
2. Live as mourning people (v. 4) who exhibit joy in hard times.
3. Live as meek people (v. 5) who humbly exhibit faithfulness instead of pride and arrogance when people seek us out.
4. Live as hungry people (vv. 6 and 8), exhibiting a desire for purity and goodness that includes integrity, honesty, and the true gospel. Then, we are seen as trustworthy.
5. Live as kind people who show mercy (v. 7) instead of being judgmental when people need help.
6. Live as peacemakers (v. 9), willing to work peacefully for unity instead of division.
7. Live as people who patiently rejoice even when persecuted and mistreated (vv. 10–12), fostering respect for the gospel.
8. Be salt (v. 13) by living in a self-controlled and consistent manner that the community will appreciate, opening more doors for ministry.
9. Be light (vv. 4–16). When Christians are seen as a light in the community, people will be drawn to them, especially as people live in darkness. The true gospel-centered church will bring glory to God, changing anyone who comes to him. This is the most significant change that can come to a community. This is why the church remains: we are to work for change in the community.

Our goal is to bring glory to God in everything we do by bringing everyone into conformity with Christ (see Col 3:23–24 and 1 Cor 10:31).

7. Remember Eternity

First Corinthians 15:51–58 puts our focus on eternity. Christ came as a change agent and commissioned us to be his change agents through the local church. We will not stay here forever; one day, we will leave to be with him and our fellow changed agents. It should be our desire to see as many people as possible in our communities changed by Christ so that they, too, spend eternity with him.

Eternity is the ultimate reason why the church should reach out to be a change agent in the community. It should be our desire to see everyone in our community saved, living a changed, Christ-indwelt life, and going to heaven. Promoting limited temporal change in a community is one thing, but the only change that will genuinely last is the life that comes when a person is changed from the inside out through the indwelling of Christ at salvation. That change will last.

Matthew 25:31–46 describes those who are genuinely saved as being known for being change agents when Christ returns. They will be those who fed the hungry, gave water to the thirsty, cared for the stranger, and invited Christ in. So why do we reach out to the community? Because Christ indwells us. Ministry should come naturally for the individual believer and the community of believers (the church). If it doesn't, one could question the legitimacy of the professed group of believers. Time after time, you see that Jesus had a high impact on his community, and in the book of Acts, you see entire communities turned upside down by those Christ indwelt. The same should be true of us.

In Luke 10:25–37 we have the story of the good Samaritan. Jesus described what a saved person should be like. We should love the Lord our God with all our heart and with all our soul and with all our strength and with all our mind, and we should love our neighbor as ourselves. So many of our churches are all about loving God, but the point here in this passage is that part of loving God is loving our neighbor. Notice the spiritual leaders ignored the needy traveler. The Samaritan represented God well by sacrificially caring for the needy man. Jesus asked this question in verse 36: "Which of these three do you think proved to be a neighbor to the man who fell into the robbers' *hands*?" The lawyer's response was telling. He said, "The one who showed mercy toward him" (v. 37).

Jesus then commanded us to follow his example in our ministry, so that we may meet the community's needs. "Go and do the same." In Village Missions, we say, "Preach the word and love the People."[5]

When we reach heaven, we will account for our lives as believers. What a great day it will be when we see the most significant change agent—the Lord Jesus Christ—and hear him say, "Well done, change agents, enter the joy of your Lord with the fellow Christ followers you have had the privilege of reaching in the rural communities you were placed in."

Conclusion and Application

God is the ultimate change agent who sent Jesus at the incarnation to provide the way to change us who were once lost and in need of his indwelling. Jesus indwells us and works through us in connection with his body on earth, the local church, as a testimony of his grace to a needy world. The reason he put us into our respective communities was and is to be to the praise of his glory.

When you think of your community, ask yourself the following questions:

- Why am I here?
- Am I connected to a local Christ-indwelt church?
- Who are the people in our community that the Lord wants me to minister to?
- Are we ministering to them like Christ would?

Our prayer should be that the light Jesus put in us and that changed us will be the light God uses to change the lives of people in our world. We must remember, "For to me, to live is Christ" (Phil 1:21).

How should we then live? Just like Christ: On mission as God's change agents in this needy world.

5. https://villagemissions.org/.

Part Two

A Theological Perspective of Rural Ministry

4

Evangelism in Rural Communities

Glenn Daman

The story is familiar and repeated frequently throughout our ministries. We attend a conference where we are challenged to reach the world with the gospel and develop a missional mindset within the church. Denominational leaders promote programs designed (and guaranteed) to bring dramatic results in the church and community. Armed with the latest research and market analysis, we are told our churches will grow if we have the right vision with the right programs. This begins with dramatic, seeker-sensitive worship that includes dazzling media displays, powerful music, and sermons that address the felt needs of the listener. We are warned that if the church is not growing, it is because it is too legalistic, old-fashioned, and governed by traditions.

Armed with the new vision for missions and motivated by the latest techniques, we go back to our church and promptly announce to the congregation that we are making substantial changes that will revolutionize our church. When the congregation resists, we criticize them for lacking a passion for the lost and failing to embrace the Great Commission. In the end, the people become frustrated, and we become discouraged, questioning our calling to ministry. We blame the people for their shortsightedness and become dejected because God seems to withhold his blessing from our ministry. Who has not doubted their calling when their church sees so little growth while the suburban megachurch is continually promoted as the ideal church with its rapid growth?

However, the problem does not lie in our failure to have the right program or music, nor in the lack of support for changes by our people. The problem lies in our inability to understand the nature of the gospel message and our responsibility to communicate it effectively in rural contexts. In an age of methodology and market strategies, evangelism has become a technique and program rather than the sovereign work of God's grace in people's hearts. Nevertheless, effective evangelism must be theologically defined and motivated rather than market-driven. Rather than looking for a market strategist, our motivation and technique for evangelism must be grounded in biblical truth. While the programs we are taught may be helpful, they are unnecessary. The gospel's message changes lives; the programs are merely avenues we can use to share the message.

Rural America: The Overlooked Mission Field

What do we see when we drive through our rural community? Often, we see morally and politically conservative people who are the "salt of the earth." They are good people who care deeply about one another and the community's needs. They are hard workers with a strong sense of right and wrong. They are "God-fearers" who believe in God and the power of hard work. They are very similar to the people who populated the rural region of Galilee during the time of Christ.

In Matt 9:35, Jesus travels through the small towns that dotted the Galilean landscape. These people believed in the Law and went to the synagogue to faithfully listen to the instructions of the rabbi. They were hard workers who cared about those around them. They sought to live righteously and according to the Torah and the traditions of the elders. They were people the disciples knew, regarded as friends and neighbors, and looked upon as religious Jews. However, in verse 36, Jesus rewrites the narrative where he calls them "harassed and helpless, like sheep without a shepherd." Jesus challenges the disciples to view them through the sight of God. From Christ's perspective, they were spiritually ravaged by sin and in need of the gospel message.

Developing a theology for evangelism begins by gaining a clear vision for the people in the local community, which involves honestly assessing their spiritual condition. We must recognize that, although rural people are often morally conservative and frequently affirm an affiliation with the local church, it does not always translate into weekly attendance or a Christ-centered life. Often, we overlook the need for rural evangelism because we fail to recognize the spiritual plight of the people within the community. Just because people are morally or religiously conservative does not mean that they are genuine disciples of Christ. As Paul states, they have the form of godliness but deny its power (2 Tim 3:5). In other words, they have the outward appearance of faith but lack genuine inward transformation of the heart. In the words of James, they possess a dead faith, for it does not affect how they act and live (Jas 2:17). Only when we begin to see our communities through the eyes of Christ will we have a genuine passion for evangelism.

The Foundation for Evangelism: The Character of God

To transform our perspective, we need to start with our understanding and perspective of the nature and character of God. When God commissioned Isaiah for his prophetic ministry to call Israel to repentance, he did not begin by calling Isaiah to be his spokesman; he started by confronting Isaiah with a vision of his own holiness. Without this vision, grace becomes cheapened, and we no longer see the necessity of repentance and transformation. Holiness is more than just an attribute of God; it is the one that unifies and governs all aspects of his nature. As Thomas Oden points out, "Holiness is not to be conceived as one trait among many other divine traits in such a way that these other traits may or may not include holiness. Rather, holiness summarizes, unifies, and integrates all the other incomparably good characters of the divine life."[1] To affirm the holiness of God is to affirm that he is not only free from the taint of sin but cannot be associated or connected with anything or anyone contaminated by sin. God hates sin and demands purity in his moral creatures.

This is what necessitates the gospel. Because God is holy, all sin, no matter how small and insignificant in our eyes, is an insult to him. In an age when we justify sin, we need to be reminded that all sin is a rejection of God. Stephen Charnock rightly points out, "A man in every sin aims to set up his own will as his rule and his own glory as the end of his actions, against the will and glory of God; and could a sinner attain his end, God would be destroyed."[2] Consequently, all sin is grounded in a secret atheism

1. Oden, *Living God*, 100.
2. Charnock, *Existence*, 1:144.

and a rejection of God's rule in our lives. We desire to be the masters of our destiny. "Man would make himself the role of God and give laws to his Creator. We are willing that God should be our benefactor, but not our ruler; we are content to admire his excellency and pay him worship, provided he will walk by our rule."[3] Only when confronted with God's holiness are we faced with the necessity for the gospel message. Only when Isaiah recognized God's holiness and had a clear understanding of his sinfulness and the people's sinfulness was he moved to respond to God's call to be God's prophetic messenger.

The holiness of God becomes the backdrop by which we see the wonder of his grace. When we see the perfection of God, we begin to see the need for salvation and the grace of God. Only when we see his holiness do we see the wonder of God's mercy revealed on the cross. When we cheapen holiness, we inevitably cheapen grace, for grace is no longer needed, and the cross becomes insignificant. Ultimately, we lose the motivation for evangelism, for the gospel becomes meaningless.

Consequently, evangelism does not start with a program; it begins with our theological perspective and the effect that sin has on us. Sin not only destroys our well-being; it destroys our relationship with God. Sin separates us from God and results in our eternal judgment. While we affirm this truth theologically and practically, we struggle because we fail to see people as inherently sinful. Consequently, we no longer see the need for the gospel. Instead of the gospel being a call to repentance, it is reduced to a tool to use for church growth. Our message becomes compromised. No longer is the gospel about repentance and the salvation of people; it becomes about how we increase the numbers. Church growth is easy; we must tell people what they want to hear. However, our task is not to increase the church's attendance; it is to communicate the gospel to people. Evangelism is telling people what they do not want to hear so that they might do the one thing that is contrary to their sinful nature. Our calling is to confront people with the reality of their sins so that they might embrace the wonder of God's grace and surrender to his sovereign rule in their lives. It is confronting sinful people with the holy God and pointing them to the grace that he offers.

3. Charnock, *Existence*, 1:190.

The Necessity of Evangelism: The Divine Mandate

Jesus makes it clear that the task of church growth is not our responsibility. In Matt 16:18, Christ takes responsibility for the growth of the church. It is he, not us, that brings the growth. Paul affirms this truth in his letter to the church at Corinth: "I planted, Apollos watered, but God gave the growth. So, neither he who plants nor he who waters is anything, but only God who gives the growth. He who plants and he who waters are equal, and each shall receive his wages according to his labor. For we are God's fellow workers; you are God's field, God's building" (1 Cor 3:6–9). If it is not our responsibility to grow the church, then what is our calling? The answer is found in the Great Commission. Our task is to make disciples of all nations (Matt 28:19–20). We are to take the gospel message to every nook and cranny of the inhabited world (Acts 1:8) and call people to be disciples of Christ. People can only embrace the gospel when it is communicated to them, and it can only be communicated when people are sent to proclaim the message (Rom 10:23–25).

The question that confronts us is this: who does the sending? The answer is God! Taking the gospel to rural people is not a denominational obligation but a divine mandate. When we overlook or minimize rural ministry because it wastes denominational resources, we undermine the mission God has given us. In the Great Commission, Christ calls us to proclaim the gospel to all people, even those living in Barrow, Alaska, or McMurdo Station on Ross Island, Antarctica.

Rural ministry as a denominational priority is not an economic issue or a question of the best use of ecclesiastical resources to achieve the most outstanding results. It is a theological issue grounded in the Great Commission. Rural communities must remain a priority for the church simply because it is a priority for God. People in rural areas need the gospel's message to obtain the salvation that Christ offers.

The church's presence in rural communities is essential to God because rural people are invaluable to him. If Christ was willing to die for them, how much more should we be willing to serve them? We must focus on rural ministry for no other reason than the command of Christ to go into all the world.

The greatest danger in the renewed focus on rural ministry we see today is that it merely becomes a fad rather than a theological mandate. Harold Longenecker rightly points out what happens when our focus shifts from the gospel's advancement to the growth of numbers:

> This, it appears, would be a sufficiently loud call for an aggressive evangelistic program in rural America. However, the scattered nature of the population, which almost precludes the building of huge churches and the small size of the existing rural churches, has dampened the enthusiasm of many. Since our approaches to church ministry are geared to the larger church, the small ones continue with little assistance. Relatively few men will give themselves to a lifetime of service in a rural church.[4]

The church's mission demands that we recognize the need for a renewed missionary effort to reach rural America. If we are more concerned about numbers and recognition than lost individuals, we have forgotten the nature of the gospel and the Great Commission. Longenecker continues, "In America's small towns and rural areas, there is still a need for those who are prepared to take the gospel at whatever personal cost, by whatever possible means, and thus to form a local fellowship of believers that will stand as a permanent witness to God and his grace."[5] The Great Commission is not about success, accomplishments, and recognition but about taking the gospel to each individual, wherever that individual might live.

The Process of Evangelism: A Movement Rather than an Event

We live in an age where we demand instantaneous results. Throughout my ministry, I have lost count of the times I received advertisements promising that if I implemented a particular program, we could double our Sunday school in six months. We become discouraged and disheartened if we do not see immediate, dramatic results. The same is true in our evangelistic efforts in rural communities. We see evangelism as an event rather than a process. We want instant results instead of engaging in a lengthy process.

Throughout Scripture, we find that the work of evangelism is described in terms of a process. Jesus points to this in the parable of the sower (Matt 12:1–9; Mark 4:1–9; Luke 8:4–8). While we often focus on the various results, we fail to recognize the implied time inherent in the process. When a farmer goes out to plant a field, he does not drive the combine into the field behind the drill. While the harvest is the goal, much more is involved before the harvest is ready. Before the seed can even be planted, the soil

4. Longenecker, *Building Town*, 26.

5. Longenecker, *Building Town*, 30.

must be prepared, for without proper tillage, a harvest is impossible. Even after the seed is planted, the harvest is still months away. The seed must germinate, the plant must develop, and the kernels must form. The field is ready for harvest only when the crop has matured and ripened. All this is implied in the story. Before the harvest, the soil must be prepared through relationships with the disciples of Christ; the gospel must be presented; the Holy Spirit must begin the gracious work of softening a hardened heart; and people must grow in their understanding of the gospel and the implications it has for their personal lives.

The process from the planting of the seed to the development of the harvest is also hinted at by Paul in 1 Cor 3. Some plant the seed of the gospel, while others water the seed. Some share the gospel with a person, while others assist in the growth of the individual's understanding before the gospel comes to full fruition in the person's life. In rural ministry, we often do not see immediate results. We get discouraged because we plan poorly attended events and obtain no visible results. We fail to recognize that it takes time to connect with people. This is especially true in rural communities. People are already aware of the church, and they have already decided not to attend. Therefore, an invitation to attend a special service is often disregarded and met with resistance. To break down the wall of resistance, two essential ingredients must exist in our gospel presentation.

First, preparing the soil is grounded in relationships, for it is by personally connecting with people that we break down the wall of resistance to the gospel. It necessitates becoming involved in the community's social life. The old cliche is true that people do not care how much you know until they know how much you care. In rural communities, people are suspicious of strangers. They are reluctant to embrace an outsider. Before they will listen to us, they must first accept and trust us. Trust can only be built through personal connection. Throughout his ministry, Jesus spent time building relationships with sinners. The one accusation that the religious leaders could rightfully bring against Jesus was that he was a friend to sinners (Matt 11:19; Luke 7:34). Jesus did not just preach a message on the hills of Galilee; he also visited people in their homes, socializing with them (Luke 19:1–10) and sharing a meal with them. Evangelism is not just a sermon preached in the pulpit; it is a message communicated through our dealings with the people. We gain a hearing in the community by becoming engaged in the community. Effective evangelism requires us to be integrated into the community's social capital, gaining their trust so that they will listen to our message.

Second, preparing the soil requires a visible demonstration of the gospel in our lives that provides a context for the gospel's authenticity to be fully revealed to others. Before people hear the gospel, we need to show them the reality of the gospel in our own lives. Peter implies this when he states, "Always be prepared to make a defense to anyone who asks you for a reason for the hope that is in you" (1 Pet 3:15). They see in us the difference the gospel makes in our lives as we face the same struggles and issues they encounter; they see we have the confidence and hope that are lacking in their lives. In our lives, we give context to the message of the gospel by demonstrating the transformational nature of the gospel. This draws them to the gospel as they face the hopelessness of their own lives.

The Power of the Gospel

The mantra of modern evangelism is that we need to have the right program, methodologies, and forms of worship. Consequently, we go from one seminar to another, each promoting the latest and greatest programs and methods. When people do not flock to our church, we point to several reasons. We are not the most eloquent speakers. We do not have a dynamic worship team. We do not have multiple ministries to meet the people's perceived needs. We do not have the facilities to attract people. As a result, we feel inadequate and ill-equipped. In the quietness of our minds, we often fall prey to the "if only . . . then . . ." mentality. If only we had a dynamic worship team, then people would come. If only we could be more entertaining in our messages, people would respond. If we had more people to develop and plan programs, people would be saved. And the list goes on. Ultimately, we feel inadequate for evangelism. Why do another evangelistic event when it is already destined to fail?

The problem is not in what we don't have, but in our failure to understand what we do have. The power of the gospel is not based on what we bring to the presentation. The power of the gospel is found in the gospel itself. This is not to say the programs and methods we are taught are not of any value. Many of the programs are helpful tools in communicating the gospel. However, we must recognize that the gospel's advancement is not dependent upon these tools. We may use the tools when they are gospel-driven and culturally relevant, but we must acknowledge that, in the end, it is the message itself that has the power to change lives rather than the tools and methods we use.

The gospel stands on its own. In Rom 1:16, Paul states, "For I am not ashamed of the gospel: it is the power of God for salvation to everyone who believes to the Jew first and also to the Greek." In other words, the transforming power necessary to effect salvation and bring the radical shift in life does not come from us but from the gospel itself. Evangelism is never about the program; it is all about the message. For Paul, the reliance on programs, techniques, and oratory skills only served to undermine the gospel rather than give power to the gospel. In 1 Cor 2:1–5, Paul deliberately avoided "lofty words or wisdom" and the reliance upon "plausible words of wisdom." Instead, he relied upon the simplicity of the gospel, for he sought to make followers of Christ rather than followers of him. In our quest for popularity and success in ministry, we become more focused on getting followers of us rather than followers of Christ. We can start to rely upon our abilities rather than the Holy Spirit's intrinsic power working through the gospel's message. We must never forget that the gospel's message is the foundation for all evangelism. Our task is not to bring people to the gospel through our techniques but to bring the message to people so that it might penetrate their hearts and transform them into faithful disciples of Christ. Apart from the gospel message, there is nothing more needed for effective evangelism.

The Centrality of Relationships

The first question we often ask when seeking to evangelize the rural community is: "How do we share the gospel with people who already know about the church and have already decided not to attend?" Consequently, when we invite them to a program, they do not come. After several attempts at different programs, we became discouraged. Ultimately, we conclude that our community is closed to the gospel. However, the problem is not the community; the problem is our methodology. As we have already pointed out, but must reiterate again, the key to reaching rural communities is not found in programs, but in the development of relationships. Within rural communities, trust is crucial for gaining a hearing through which we can share the gospel. A farmer buys machinery from the salesman he knows and trusts rather than a salesman from a distant town who emails or calls him on the phone. A business transaction is based upon a handshake rather than a signed legal document.

While the gospel transforms the person, our relationship with people gains a hearing with them. The most powerful tool in evangelism is not a dynamic program but a personal connection. The best evangelistic tool is not an evangelism explosion or developing a seeker sensitive church; it is a cup of coffee shared with unchurched people at the local watering hole. I have heard it said that in rural areas, it takes gallons of bad coffee to see one soul come to Christ.

The Transformation and Implication of the Gospel

To understand evangelism, we also need to affirm the purpose of the gospel. The gospel is not just the story of redemption and salvation from sin. Indeed, this is central but not all-encompassing. Too often, the gospel is presented merely as a means of saving people from hell. But the Great Commission is not just about obtaining freedom from judgment. In Matt 28:19, the verb *go* is a contemporaneous or complementary participle that completes the idea of action expressed in the main verb, which is the present imperative to "make disciples of all nations." The purpose of evangelism is to bring the complete transformation of people who live in full obedience to Christ. As Philip Adam points out, at times, we approach the gospel and evangelism with the question, "'What is the irreducible minimum of the gospel the unbeliever needs to hear?' rather than 'What is the fullness of the gospel God has revealed?'"[6] Evangelism is not just a call to repentance to avoid hell; it is a call to complete transformation to become like Christ. Redemptive faith inevitably leads to a life of obedience to Christ (John 14:15, 21, 23). To embrace the gospel is to develop a spirituality marked by faith and obedience in every area of life.[7]

In Romans, Paul takes it a step further. The call of the gospel is to become part of the community of God's people so that they might become transformed in Christ to become part of the bride of Christ. In Rom 1–8, Paul sets forth the nature of the gospel as a personal response of faith to the redemptive work of Christ. However, in chapters 9–16, he sets forth the application of the gospel. The gospel results in surrendering ourselves to God within the context of the body of Christ. Having responded to the gospel, we are now to respond in obedience to God by using our spiritual gifts in the mutual service of the church (see also Rom 6:1–7 and 1 Cor

6. Adam, *Hearing*, 25.

7. Adam, *Hearing*, 90.

12).[8] James, likewise, sees the implication of the gospel in relationship with the community of believers. For James, redemptive faith is a transformative faith that is lived in the community of faith where there is mutual care and concern (Jas 2:14–26).

The necessity of the gospel *for* rural communities results in the necessity of the church *in* rural communities. The rural church is both the basis for evangelism and the goal of evangelism. The church's presence in rural areas is not just a denominational issue; it is a profoundly theological issue grounded in the gospel and the goal of evangelism. To be passionate about reaching rural communities for Christ is to establish and strengthen the rural church as a reflection of Christ. To have a theological mandate for evangelizing rural areas results in a theological mandate for establishing, maintaining, and strengthening the rural church.

Never Devalue the Value of One

For Philip, the vision must have been confusing (Acts 8:26–39). The disciples were enjoying enormous success in their evangelistic efforts in Jerusalem. The church was growing, programs were being developed, and outreach was conducted in other population centers in the region. So effective was the ministry that even today, the church in Jerusalem remains a subject of study and analysis by students of church growth. Things were happening, people were getting saved, and the Holy Spirit was moving. Yet amid all this success, Philip received a vision to go into the solitary desert of the southern wilderness of Israel. The Greek is concise: "Arise and go south . . . it is a desert." In other words, leave the place where the ministry is growing and go to a place without people.

Phillip was told to leave where they were enjoying great success in their evangelistic work, to go to a place entirely inappropriate for effective ministry.[9] It did not make sense. The church in Jerusalem was exploding, and Philip was told to leave and go into the wilderness, void of anyone. When Philip arrived in the region, he must have questioned his vision, for there was no caravan of people and no tribe of Bedouins traveling through to greet him. Instead, all he found was one individual from a foreign country. But as Philip saw the man, the Holy Spirit made it clear that Philip was to approach this lone man.

8. Adam, *Hearing*, 88.

9. Peterson, *Acts of the Apostles*, 293.

We know the results. The individual (who is not even named) was an official of the queen of Ethiopia and was reading the prophecies of Isa 53. In response to his questions, Philip shared the gospel implications of the prophecies of Isaiah. As a result, the official embraced the message. No program or dynamic service was employed, just a simple message. Church tradition suggests this person became the first evangelist in Africa and may have been responsible for establishing or expanding the Coptic church in Africa.[10]

In rural ministry, we often feel like Philip in the wilderness. Why should we go to a small, insignificant church in a tiny, forgotten town in the middle of nowhere? Is that not a waste of our time, energy, and resources? Indeed, from a career perspective, it makes no sense. Is it not better to become part of a growing urban ministry where our skills and education can be better served? However, God does not place value on numbers. He places value on individuals.

Early in his ministry, Jesus was gaining popularity and recognition in the urban regions of Judea. Instead of capitalizing on this popularity, he left the region to go to a small village called Sychar in the undesirable region of Samaria. Here, he had a divine appointment with a troubled woman. For Jesus, this woman was more important than the growth of his popularity (John 4:1–6). This is the nature of God's grace and the nature of the gospel. Christ did not just come to save the masses but to deliver individuals. One lost sheep is more valuable than the ninety-nine sheep in the fold (Matt 18:10–14). Christ came to die for each person.

We need to take the gospel to rural (and urban) communities because of the infinite value God places upon each person. We may only reach one person with the gospel in our whole ministry. However, for that one person, our ministry has eternal significance. In God's redemptive program, the one individual we reach with the gospel is just as important as the masses reached at a Billy Graham crusade. In developing a theology of evangelism for rural ministry, at the center must be the recognition that the value of one individual in the sight of God is worth a lifetime of ministry. If all we reach is one person for Christ, our ministry is still thriving. In God's economy, the value of one is of infinite importance. If we devalue the importance of reaching one person with the gospel, we ultimately devalue Christ's work on the cross. The ultimate motivation of evangelism is not "how many" but "who." The salvation of one person is still worthy of the celebration of heaven (Luke 15:10). If the angels break out in glorious praise when one

10. Hubbard, "Ethiopian Eunuch," 346.

person embraces the gospel, how much more should we rejoice and value each person who comes to Christ because of our ministry? We can never devalue the value God places on each person who hears and responds to the gospel.

5

Loving God Where Your Feet Are

A Theological Rationale for the Local Church

Charles E. Cotherman

For decades, Bud Smith's Store stood at the crossroads village of Nineveh, Pennsylvania. Behind the two-story white columns, which offered a formality juxtaposed to the surrounding fields and modest houses, a man and his wife earned a living and built a community by selling parcels of land for new homes. Unlike the dollar stores that dot rural communities today, Bud and Thelma sold everything from work boots and guns to gas, meat, fresh produce, and penny candy. Located between my grandfather's two farmsteads, it offered my dad and uncle a convenient high school job. Thirty years later, it provided my brother and me with a destination worth a four-mile bike ride.

If you live in a rural area, you know where this is going. About twenty-five years ago, Bud's Store closed. The Smiths' age and lack of a successor were contributing factors, but just as significant was the nearby construction (almost simultaneously in two neighboring towns) of another store that bore its founder's name. As it turned out, Sam Walton had discovered a more efficient way to meet the needs of communities like Nineveh.

What does this story have to do with the rural church? In some ways, rural churches have followed a trajectory that is both similar and distinct from that of mom-and-pop businesses. Many rural communities that have lost their general stores, businesses, and family farms still have main streets and country roads dotted with steeple-topped churches. Nineveh is a case in point. The country church just down the road from what was Bud's Store is thriving today.

Many small congregations, however, could hardly be described as thriving. Budgetary shortfalls and a failure to replace aging members of the congregation who pass away are common struggles for many rural congregations. Other challenges are more subtle. While financial records, annual baptisms, and weekly attendance numbers are hard to miss, a less identifiable and more universal threat to local congregations comes from a shared set of cultural assumptions that prioritize efficiency above nearly all else. To maintain a vision of the importance of local congregations in areas with small populations and seemingly limited potential, we must face the subtle power of this cultural value head-on.

Contextualizing Our Culture's Emphasis on Efficiency

Americans have long valued pragmatism and sought fast-tracks to progress. Early colonists blended idealism (they were founding a "city on the hill" in a "new world") and realism (first, they had to build houses, plant crops, and make sure they didn't die of starvation or disease in the wilderness). This heady blend of pragmatism and idealism shaped the history, culture, and religious practices of the new nation.

By the late nineteenth century, the disappearance of the frontier and the increasing influence of the Industrial Revolution gave the drive for pragmatic solutions and efficiency a more explicit and culturally dominant role.[1] The nationwide push for industrialization offered new metrics for quantifying productivity and the value of individual workers.

The name commonly associated with this shift is Fredrick W. Taylor (1856–1915). An engineer from Philadelphia, Pennsylvania, Taylor developed a process of "practical scientific management" that sought to "reorganize and standardize workers' jobs."[2] Beginning in the 1880s, Taylor began studying individual worker motions and the time needed to carry them out to develop a "'one best way'—for the completion of each task."[3] As historian Jacquelyn Dowd Hall and her team of authors demonstrate in their

1. The 1890 US Census demonstrated that America no longer included a frontier.
2. Hall et al., *Like a Family*, 204.
3. Hall et al., *Like a Family*, 204.

book *Like a Family: The Making of a Southern Cotton Mill World*, these "Taylorisms" had an immediate and far-reaching impact on industries like the manufacturing of textiles.[4] Propelled forward by newly hired mill consultants, who sought to "recommend efficiencies in every aspect of production from bookkeeping methods to machine loads and pay scales,"[5] mills dehumanized their working conditions. They downplayed the value of skilled laborers who had developed a lifetime of expertise.

The push for efficiency dominated much of American culture by the early twentieth century. Not all changes were bad. Today, we appreciate (and probably take for granted) the efficiency of septic lines and the electric grid. However, while we can acknowledge the importance of some changes that accompanied the social and infrastructural reforms of the Progressive Era, the early decades of the twentieth century also demonstrated that efficiency could be used in ways that compromised human dignity and personal flourishing. The First World War demonstrated how efficient we had become at killing our enemies—a point reinforced ad nauseam throughout the remainder of the twentieth century.

By the early 1960s, when much of the world lived under the terrifying shadow of another highly efficient weapon—the atomic bomb—French sociologist Jacques Ellul identified this totalizing power of efficiency as the hallmark of "a technological society." For Ellul, it was not technology or technological innovation that made a society "technological"; instead, it was its thoroughgoing adoption of "technique." In his 1964 book, *The Technological Society*, Ellul detailed how technique—and its unabashed emphasis on ever-increasing efficiency—had become "a universal language."[6]

Technique's influence has only grown in the decades since Ellul first identified its powerful grip on the modern world. As Alan Noble points out in his book *You Are Not Your Own*, when "efficiency becomes the greatest good," we are left with a world that feels "out of step with our basic humanity."[7] As Western culture abandons a belief in overarching truth claims or a shared moral compass, the technique's relentless and dehumanizing drive for efficiency fills the vacuum. In a culture devoid of shared value systems, most implicitly agree on the value of efficiency. But efficiency has a cost. Since efficiency always implies competition, we find ourselves in a

4. Hall et al., *Like a Family*, 204–12.
5. Hall et al., *Like a Family*, 205.
6. Ellul, *Technological Society*, 132.
7. Noble, *You Are Not Your Own*, 17, 52.

constant rat race to outperform others and demonstrate our value.[8] Those who cannot keep up fall behind, and society moves on.

The Church in a Technological Society

The rural church did not escape the expanding push for efficiency. By the first decades of the twentieth century, efforts were underway to bring rural churches under an ecclesiological variation of Taylorism. Theodore Roosevelt's National Commission on Country Life issued a 1909 report highlighting the positive contributions of rural congregations to their communities. Still, the report also found rural areas to have more churches than the commission deemed necessary.[9] Based on this assessment, the members of the Commission on Country Life called for the "consolidation of denominational churches" within counties as well as the creation of union churches, which consisted of the merger of congregations from differing denominations into one congregation.[10] They also recommended what they considered an optimal church-to-population ratio—one church per thousand residents.[11] Taylorism's one-best-way approach was also applied to the church.

While many of these early efforts to quantify the efficiency of rural congregations were carried out by denominational or governmental entities, the drive for efficiency became less institutionalized and more pervasive over time. In post-war America, a push for efficiency within the local church was often led by a revolving group of church growth consultants and expert communicators who built large ministries by systematically appropriating business techniques and large media platforms. But as local churches looked to top-selling Christian authors and famous television preachers, they witnessed a new kind of efficiency that rewarded those who had won the competition for market share. Even as smaller churches looked to examples in worship or church leadership they could never hope to match, these models provided the standard against which local churches often had to compete in the eyes of their congregants and even in their self-estimation. No wonder the temptation toward church consolidation and megachurches has been so compelling. Like Walmart, these larger churches have harnessed the power of efficiency to significant effect.

8. Noble, *You Are Not Your Own*, 61–82.
9. Jung et al., *Rural Ministry*, 42–43.
10. Jung et al., *Rural Ministry*, 43.
11. Jung et al., *Rural Ministry*, 43.

In a culture obsessed with efficiency, rural churches need a theological rationale not only for determining the contours of ministry but also for justifying their existence. In a bigger-is-better culture, small churches in small places face persistent questions. Why should small churches not simply consolidate into larger congregations for greater specialization? Do small places even need a local church? Why not establish a large hub church in each region, adopting an approach similar to corporate chains? Are small churches a poor use of ministry resources? In our current cultural moment, these are daunting questions. Fortunately, the story of God's work among his people offers those of us serving in small places and congregations exactly what we need to serve, right where we are—confidence.

Creation as a Theological Rationale for the Local Church

To get a glimpse of God's intention for creation and humanity, we need to look at the sections of Scripture that describe life before the fall (Gen 1–2) and after sin (Rev 21–22). As Glenn Daman noted in the introduction, eschatology matters for pastoral ministry. So does the story of creation! While the creation account never mentions the church, it lays a crucial theological foundation for our work in local communities.

Intentional Inefficiency in Creation

The first thing worth noting when we examine the creation account is how *intentionally inefficient* it is. This may seem counterintuitive. Creating with a few words ("Let there be light" in Gen 1:3) is about as efficient a means of creating as one could imagine. But against the background of God's omnipotence, the planned inefficiency of Genesis stands out. God could have created everything with a word in one unfathomably efficient moment, but God chose not to create that way. Instead, God opted for a multi-stage process, drawn out over time, with an intentionality that gradually built creation by laying one creative act expertly upon the one that came before. At the end of it all, God, who is infinitely powerful and shares none of the physical constraints of his creation, chooses to model inefficiency once more by making rest the culmination of his creative work. All of this, in its individual stages and its completion, God repeatedly describes as "very good."

God's interaction with humanity also demonstrates his intentional inefficiency. Throughout Gen 2, the reader encounters a God who values the slow work of relationship building over simply getting the job done. Rather than naming the animals (as their Creator) or tending the garden himself (as the expert gardener), God chooses to enter a relationship with Adam. By entrusting Adam with key tasks, God slows down enough to help Adam step into his calling. Even when Adam and Eve lose sight of their high calling and heed the serpent's advice to doubt God's goodness and concern for them, God does not give up on them or change his willingness to allow humanity to tend the earth. Amid the messiness of real life, God remains committed to cultivating a relationship with humanity. Humanity's task gets harder after sin, but the primary contours of the cultural mandate stay the same.

The Gift of Creation

At every stage, the process of creation is a gift. God does not need creation or humans to tend to creation. Out of love, God chooses to work at the speed his creatures can handle, focusing on relationships, not efficiency.

If you have ever worked with someone far superior (or inferior) to you in ability, you may have had a glimpse at what this type of intentional inefficiency looks like. I am an amateur carpenter from a long line of experienced carpenters. Over the years, I have had the opportunity to work alongside carpenters in my family and professional contractors in various settings. Sometimes, the master builder was willing to stop long enough to bring me along, training me as I worked to learn the trade. At other times, efficiency won out, and I took the role of a passive observer (or gofer) while the true expert completed the task faster than a novice like me could. We face this trade-off between efficiency and relationship all the time. (Any parent who has ever inwardly groaned when a child asked to help with a household chore knows the struggle is real!)

The first few chapters of Genesis—not to mention God's entire journey with his people from the call of Abram in Gen 12 to today—demonstrate that the God of the universe is willing to slow down, be present, and value the process of building a relationship over simply accomplishing the task most efficiently.

This attribute of God's care for creation can provide rural pastors and congregations with a sense of confidence in fulfilling the work they are called to do. Rural churches are usually not built for efficiency. They seldom rely on the fine-tuned systems or specialization that a technological society values. What rural churches can offer, however, is an opportunity to be truly known within the church and the larger community. This is something pastor Ronnie Martin noticed immediately when he moved from the sprawl of Southern California to a small town in northern Ohio. Accustomed to seeing "anonymous faces everywhere" he went, after several years pastoring in a small town he found himself encountering "multiple people I've known for years in almost every conceivable juncture."[12] Many small-town pastors can identify. There is seldom a quick trip to the store. On the way to grab a gallon of milk, we see congregants, neighbors, and our children's teachers. Conversations and times of prayer in the aisle often ensue.

Like the act of creation, which took time and entailed potential complications and relational risks, there are faster ways to get our goods than visiting a local store. (A purchase from Amazon comes with no chance of running into that chatty church member in town.) Similarly, the church in much of the Western world faces a temptation to divorce basic features of congregational life from actual relationships. Why employ a local preacher when a sermon on YouTube or a podcast from an expert may offer a superior "product" on a timeline of one's choosing? Why support a small church in a town losing population when a longer commute will take you to a larger church that functions as a one-stop Christian resource center? When faced with these questions, God's willingness to sacrifice efficiency for relationships offers a compelling case for prioritizing relationships within the local church and the surrounding community.

Locality and Creation

Another instructive element of the creation narrative for churches is the boundedness of Adam and Eve's call. Whereas their fruitfulness and ensuing multiplication would eventually fill the earth, in the immediate moment, God calls them to a task that is bounded and local. God designates one specific place—a garden—and puts the man in it to work. There is an entire earth to care for, but God calls Adam to take care of this one corner. Of course, Adam's work in that small locale can touch the rest if God desires (e.g., God brings the animals to Adam to name). But the extent

12. Griggs and Martin, *Pastoring Small Towns*, 96.

of Adam's influence is God's prerogative, not Adam's. Adam's call is to be faithful where his feet are.

This call to boundedness in place endures. Today, embodied and localized faithfulness may be more critical than ever. As sociologist James Davidson Hunter notes in his widely read book *To Change the World: The Irony, Tragedy, & Possibility of Christianity in the Late Modern World*, a commitment to "faithful presence" in the places we inhabit every day is as formative as necessary. As Hunter notes, "Against the limitless horizon of a will that is ever seeking its own fulfillment and pleasure, faithful presence calls believers to yield their will to God and to nurture and cultivate the world where God has placed them . . . to attend to the people and places that they experience directly."[13] While Hunter addresses his charge to all believers, the localized faithfulness and stewardship of place over time that he calls the church to is well-suited to the experience of rural congregations.

Reaching for More

As powerful as the call to localized faithfulness is in Gen 2, the next chapter demonstrates that our connection to faithfulness in place is also fragile. In Gen 3, the serpent entices Eve with the same two lies our enemy still uses to sabotage our faithfulness today. First, the serpent asks if God really said what Eve thought he said. Next, the serpent calls Eve to doubt God's care for her. According to the serpent, God is holding out on her, keeping something good from her. Soon, Eve and Adam (who was also with her) swallowed the lie and the fruit. They choose to push against the limits and the relational process God has given them. Theirs is a quest for a more efficient way to get what they want. In the process, they lose much of what they had.

Pastors, churches, and entire movements can still become entangled in seeking quick fixes that lead them to neglect the places and people God has called them to serve. Sometimes, our ambition drives us on. In other cases, it may be our insecurity. Do we really think this place or this church matters? Do we really believe that we matter to God? Can I trust God to provide for me and my family here? Wouldn't it simply be better—more efficient and more eternally significant—to move on to the next place or to consolidate churches so we can reach more people?

Most rural pastors know that these are not hypothetical questions. When I told my admittedly risk-averse father ten years ago that Aimee and

13. Hunter, *To Change the World*, 253.

I were planning to move back to rural western Pennsylvania from an upwardly mobile university town to plant a church in Oil City, he promptly told me not to do it. I can still remember him saying, "There's no money there. How will you support your family?" Was Oil City too small and too economically challenged? We had to ask and answer these questions. Ultimately, God reminded us of the value of small places and his ability to provide for them. We planted Oil City Vineyard Church in 2016, and God has provided every step of the way.

The Incarnation: A Theological Rationale for the Local Church

As important as the creation account in Gen 1–3 is for helping us understand the character of God and the world as we know it, the most robust rationale for local churches and life within the limits of our creaturely finitude comes not from the first Adam but from the second.

In the opening verses of his Gospel, John undeniably signals that the life and ministry of Jesus is the beginning of a new creation.[14] Echoing the "in the beginning" of Gen 1, John frames the incarnation of Jesus as a watershed moment in cosmic history. The One who was "in the beginning with God" (John 1:2) and through whom "all things were made" (v. 3) has now "become flesh and dwelt among us" (v. 14). As N. T. Wright notes, "John . . . is, at his very heart, a theologian of creation."[15]

John is not alone among New Testament authors in seeing the connection between the incarnation and new creation. Paul picks up on the theme more than once in his epistles by describing Jesus as a "second" or "last" Adam. Unlike the first Adam, whose unfaithfulness brought sin and death to the world, the second Adam, Jesus, chose faithfulness and thereby extended the gift of life to humanity and renewal to creation (Rom 5:12–21; 8:18–25; 1 Cor 15:42–49).

Presence and Limits in the Incarnation

From the earliest gatherings of Christ followers to the oldest Christian creeds, the reality of Christ's incarnation and the events it makes possible

14. Wright, *Resurrection of the Son*, 667–68.

15. Wright, *Resurrection of the Son*, 667.

(e.g., his ministry, death, resurrection, and ascension) have formed the core of Christian faith, teaching, and hope. There is an unavoidable situatedness in place and time within creedal statements that claim Jesus was "born of the virgin Mary" and "suffered under Pontius Pilate." Jesus comes to us not as a disembodied spirit or a fleeting sensation but as an embodied human, indeed as *fully* human as he is *fully* God.

The implications of this reality are momentous. At its core, the incarnation makes a case for embracing the overlap of spiritual and physical realities in the earthy situatedness—and inherent complexities—of culture, place, and time. Whereas it might be more efficient to mandate, as Islam does, that all believers read Scripture and pray in one language, the incarnation demonstrates God's willingness to translate his message to local contexts, including local languages.[16] (As Rev 7:9 reminds us, this diversity is a lasting feature of the kingdom of God.) It might seem easier to figure out the "one best way" to efficiently proclaim the gospel on a large scale, far removed from the intricacies of particular people and places. Still, in the incarnation, we see God with the dust of Galilean roads and Samaritan towns on his feet. We see God taking time to understand the local culture of unpretentious rural villages and then telling parables suited to the everyday experiences of those who live there. Through it all, Jesus works within the limitations of embodied humanity. He did not visit every village in Galilee, nor did he heal every sick person in Israel. He was faithfully present to his Father and people with the geographic limitations of place.

No aspect of Jesus's ministry strategy was planned around efficiency or the "one best way" to distribute the most spiritual goods in the least amount of time. (Ask yourself, would it have been better if Jesus had come in the twenty-first century so he could have maximum impact as an Instagram influencer?) In fact, by the end of Jesus's life, someone looking for a solid return on investment would have been disappointed. All the grand prophecies seemed misplaced. Most of Jesus's life was spent in obscurity, so much so that we know almost nothing about the twenty-eight years or so between his flight to Egypt and his baptism. When he does emerge on the scene, he travels slowly; he often spends time in small towns and rural areas and embraces frequent interruptions from children, sinners, and virtually anyone who can get near him with a need. Jesus also demonstrates a remarkable level of patience with twelve men who are generally a bit slow on the uptake. Through it all, we see God in the flesh demonstrating the same intentional

16. Sanneh, *Translating the Message*, 33–55.

inefficiency that prioritizes relationships and careful attention to the hopes, hurts, and needs of the everyday people and places around him.

It is a marvelously inefficient act of love, a recognition.

A Hunger for Presence: How the Local Church Helps Us Be More Human

In the first pages of *The Life We're Looking For: Reclaiming Relationship in a Technological World*, Andy Crouch notes that "recognition is the first human quest." For a newborn baby, the first few seconds of life are spent searching for a face that returns its gaze.[17] To be recognized—to have a gaze returned—is to be in relationship, and to be in relationship is one of the most fundamental aspects of our humanity. Before the fall, humans were in a relationship first with God, then with creation and each other. For Adam and Eve, as for all of us, sin brought a breakdown of the relationship on every level.

It was up to a second Adam—the incarnate Son of God—to redeem what sin had tarnished and restore the relationship between humans and God, humans and each other, and humans and the places they called home. Jesus's incarnation was the ultimate act of recognition. In the incarnation, Jesus truly saw us, not from a satellite image or thirty thousand feet but from ground level. As Eugene Peterson said, "The Word became flesh and blood and moved into the neighborhood" (John 1:14 MSG).

It is hard to deny that we live in an increasingly inhuman world, where screens and the virtual realities they beckon us toward are attuned to the consumerist potential of each user with logarithmic efficiency. It feels like for every call to shop local—to pay attention to the people and places around us—another Amazon box smiles up at us from our doorsteps, and another Dollar General, with its purposefully decontextualized efficiency, opens nearby.

In this context, the local church can function as a signpost of the kingdom of God by helping Christians and their neighbors learn to embrace the God-given and God-sanctioned limitations and potential of their humanity. In a rootless age, Christians can embrace the places they call home, knowing that God loves these places and can bring good out of them. Christians can and should do this on an individual and family level, but we should also be involved in this local faithfulness on a congregational level. Like parents

17. Crouch, *Life We're Looking For*, 3.

who choose to attend their children's sporting events and school functions, a congregation's decision to be present in its community communicates something powerful about the value of a place and its people.

Choosing to put down roots or to keep showing up in the same place year after year may seem like an inefficient use of time and resources. But remember, with God, the question "Can anything good come from Nazareth" (or from Oil City, Pennsylvania; Aberdeen, South Dakota; or whatever corner of the world you call home) is always met with a resounding yes! God's choice to place finite humans in his creation with the command to steward one corner of it reminds us that none of us—as individuals or as a congregation—is called to do it all. A "one best way" does not exist for humanity, nor does it exist for the church. No matter how loudly the siren of efficiency calls or how many church growth strategies we encounter, we will never be able to mass-produce a more efficient ministry model than a spirit-empowered human presence. God intends for us to pay attention to the local context in which we serve so we can recognize his presence in every place we cast our eyes or set our feet. Wherever we find ourselves, God has been there first, planting the flag of his love and tending his creation with the attentiveness of a master gardener.

What the church can do is look to the incarnation—the beginning of God's wondrous new creation—as a model of local attentiveness that combines our finitude with the unlimited potential of God. The same Holy Spirit that was active in the person of Jesus now empowers God's people to be emissaries of the kingdom in every hilltop and holler and every hamlet and high-rise. In our screen-saturated and increasingly virtual world, people are hungry for presence and the recognition it brings. It is a hunger the local church is called to help fill. Filled with the Spirit of God, who chooses relationship over efficiency, the local church can draw on the theological richness of God's work in creation and the incarnation as a foundation for its attentive and faithful presence among people and in places where our society is tempted to overlook them.

Conclusion

Today, the common refrain to shop local often serves as an explicit attempt to draw our attention to the people and places around us that produce our food and populate main streets and farmers' markets. For Bud Smith's store, these calls came too late. When Bud and Thelma closed their doors, the community lost more than a store; it lost the stories that Bud and Thelma shared with those who entered, and it lost the contextualized knowledge of a people and a place that allowed Bud and Thelma to care for people as individuals, not anonymous consumers. It is more efficient to profit from anonymous consumers, but efficiency comes at a cost—namely, the loss of a relationship.

In a technological society, local churches that operate on a human scale rather than a corporate model are uniquely suited to be a prophetic voice for the goodness of geographic rootedness and relational presence. Members of local congregations bear a responsibility that goes beyond what shopping locally entails. Considering creation and the incarnation, members of local congregations are called to *live* locally, to pay attention to the stories, hopes, joys, and sorrows of the people and places surrounding them. No one church can do this alone. This is the combined call of all churches, whether they find themselves in Jerusalem, Judea, Samaria, or the ends of the earth. It is a call to be present. It is a call to be faithful. It is a chance to remind even the smallest, most seemingly forgotten places of the goodness of Immanuel, the God who is with us.

6

How Does an Outsider Become an Insider?

Ron Klassen

In Phoenix, where my wife, Roxy, and I grew up, car horns are used as angry reactions on busy streets. Soon after moving to rural Nebraska, we learned that car horns are used as friendly greetings. People in Chicago were asked how long they should wait to act if they were behind a car at a stoplight that had turned green. The consensus was two seconds. In rural Iowa, some suggested letting the light circulate one time. Imagine being a new pastor in a rural community and using a car horn that reflects your city background. Do you think it would impact your ministry?

When God moved Roxy and me to the country, we soon realized people dressed differently. Regarding my rounded-toe boots, a rancher said, "You know, a good boot will kill a cockroach in a corner."

They talked differently. *Dinner* was at noon, *supper* in the evening, and *lunch* was a between-meals snack. We learned this the hard way when we invited new friends over for what we thought was the evening meal. We learned the difference between *pickups* and *trucks*. A rancher invited me over to help "work calves." I had no idea what that meant. I began listening to agriculture radio to learn the language of farmers and ranchers.

They played differently. Their recreation was rodeoing on someone's ranch or shooting clay pigeons. I'd never even fired a gun!

I thought cross-cultural ministry happens when we cross the ocean. A man from New York City, who had served as a missionary in Irian Jaya and then as a pastor in rural North Dakota, told me that the cultural differences he encountered in North Dakota were just as challenging.

Cultural differences can catch us unawares. They can be embarrassing. One day, as I was riding with a rancher, trying to get on his wavelength, I pointed and said, "Those are nice-looking cows." It turns out they weren't cows; they were steers.

Many people are moving to the country today—a positive development, as rural America has been experiencing population loss for years. But it's also bad news for some because these newcomers aren't like them. Because of increasingly diverse populations, towns a few miles apart can have vast cultural differences. Within thirty minutes of where I live in central Illinois, there's a grain elevator town, factory town, tourist town, prison town, college town, river town, and medical town.

Driving into some of these towns, it's evident that many residents are not perfectionists. Regarding my town, outsiders have said that when our streets get dirty, we don't sweep them, we repave them! Reflecting on today's increasingly diverse rural America, someone said, "If you've seen one rural town . . . you've seen one rural town."

As we compare one small town with another, inevitably, the culture that is different from ours gets the short stick. If we're not careful, we will portray a "my way is better" attitude and, in not-so-subtle ways, communicate how fortunate they are that we showed up to improve things. Cultural differences are behind many conflicts. Cultural differences can have a negative impact on newcomers, including the pastor's family. Culture shock, as it is often called, can make it challenging to have a fruitful ministry; it can lead to short tenures. Cultural differences can stymie gospel work and cause a ministry train wreck.

Yet, countless rural pastors have not only navigated cultural differences but have also grown to love their new cultures, feel at home there, and been used by God to lead thriving ministries. Fortunately, the Bible offers godly examples and guidance for skillfully bridging cultural differences.

Increasing Our Cultural IQ

Before gleaning insights from Scripture, let's drill down more on our cross-cultural understanding. Leading cultural expert David Livermore provides a helpful definition: "Culture is the beliefs, values, behaviors, customs, and attitudes that distinguish one group from another." More simply, "It's the way we do things around here."[1]

Three cultures call for the focus of those in rural ministry.[2] First is our *personal culture*. When we move to a new community, we bring not just our belongings but also our own personal culture that affects how we think, function, and relate to others. Our personal culture was formed by where we grew up, the size of our family and community, our parents' education, occupations, and socioeconomic status. It is influenced and determined by where we went to school, who we married, our work experience, the number of places we have lived and traveled, our church background, and many other factors.

Some of us are blunt and direct; we feel free to express ourselves with our car horns. Some of us get along more easily with specific segments of the population. Though I've worked behind a desk for forty years and have a doctorate, I am comfortable with blue-collar workers because I grew up in a blue-collar home. Some of us are quite steeped in a particular church tradition. I have a friend who was determined to leave his denominational roots; he planted an independent church. But if you walk into that church not knowing anything about it, you will soon conclude it was a part of that denomination because it's what the church planter knew.

What happens when we grow up in a city, our dad is in management, and we attend a megachurch . . . and then we move to a rural community, and the church we've been called to pastor has less than one hundred attending? We'll soon find that the people are different in our new church. Then, we may try to change them. And then, we may be looking for a new church!

The second is *community culture*. We find ourselves in a new town. What are the chances that our personal culture will match our new community's culture? It's rare, even if our new town is just a few miles down the road from where we grew up. We do well to ask questions that will help us get to know our community's culture: How did it come to be? Who were its first settlers? What symbols does it have (e.g., a town square, courthouse, factory smokestack, historical marker)? What are its magnets? Where and how do people play? What are its chief economic drivers? Have they

1. Livermore, *Leading with Cultural Intelligence*, 69.

2. Harold Longenecker, a former coworker of mine, first introduced me to these three cultures. I do not know if this was original with him.

changed over the years? What are its rhythms and patterns of movement? How are decisions made? Who are the honored and despised? What ethnic groups are present? What are its hurts? What battles has it fought in years past? What becomes of its sons and daughters? What perceptions do outsiders have?

Answering questions like these will enhance our cultural understanding and facilitate assimilation. Friday night football or morning coffee gatherings may be keys to cultural acceptance. A history of opposing school consolidation reveals that many do not view big as better. Observing that a large segment of the labor force works with their hands helps us understand why many do not see desk work as "real work." The fact that many are "jacks of all trades, masters of none" provides a clue about their nonperfectionistic nature. The fact that many are their own bosses, whether on their farms or in their small businesses, helps us understand why they are fiercely independent and why grassroots decision-making is the norm. Frequent, unpredictable events and setbacks, such as crop failures, adverse weather conditions, and fluctuating markets, provide insight into why there is ambivalence toward long-range planning. Unreliable income helps explain ambivalence toward budgeting.

Third is *church culture*. We dare not assume that the culture of our church matches that of the community. Rural churches can be found in cities. Subcultures in towns sometimes find each other—for example, blue-collar workers in a largely white-collar town or expressive people in a mostly stoic town. James Plueddemann writes, "The trickiest cross-cultural challenges can occur within what we think is our own culture, but in reality is a unique subculture."[3]

We do well to get to know our church by reading old bulletins and meeting minutes, talking to old-timers, and being careful observers. When was the church founded, and what prompted its formation? What are its highs and lows? What kinds of leaders has it had? Has it always been about the same size? Where is it located in town? What roles has it had in the community? What is it known for in the community?

The past can hold the key to helping a church move forward. ("It's time to build again," "Educating our children has always been important," or "We have a history of welcoming immigrants.") Being located downtown might provide a clue about who attends there: the town fathers, the long-tenured businesspeople, and the established social class. Churches on the

3. Plueddemann, *Leading Across Cultures*, 43.

edge of town might have more newcomers, younger adults, and less rooted people. Do you think you might approach pastoring these two churches differently?

A strong ethnic influence in the church, whether in its history or more recent, may have shaped its culture. Many denominations have an ethnic component that is as strong an influence as their theological distinctives. A church that has existed for some time will be rich in history and tradition—reasons for celebration and precedence to build upon while recognizing the need to be more cautious and deliberate about introducing change.

Keen observers, inquisitive natures, and deliberate learners will have an advantage in cultural understanding. A high cultural IQ is a key to successful leadership and fruitful ministry.

Addressing Cultural Differences in the Rural Landscape

One doesn't need to fly to Australia to encounter cultural differences; all we need to do is move to a rural community . . . or introduce ourselves to the new neighbors next door.[4] Of great importance, perhaps of eternal consequence, is how effectively we navigate cultural differences. Fortunately, the Bible provides help.

Foundational Prerequisites for Bridging Cultures

A Wholesome Attitude

Our attitude is revealed by our spirit when confronted with cultural differences. Note the example of the One who bridged the greatest cultural gulf ever spanned (from heaven to earth): "Have this mind among yourselves, which is yours in Christ Jesus, who, though he was in the form of God, did not count equality with God a thing to be grasped, but emptied himself, by taking the form of a servant, being born in the likeness of men" (Phil 2:5–7 NIV).

Years ago, a pastoral couple relocated from the lush mountains and forests of the Pacific Northwest to the barren Arizona desert and an isolated,

4. For a better understanding of common differences between city and rural cultures, see Wells, Giese, and Klassen, *Leading Through Change*, 23–36.

impoverished town. Recapping this experience, they told me, "We decided we were going to like it, even if we didn't."

Our inclination is not to like it. A wholesome attitude will decide otherwise. Paul reminds us that attitude is a choice: "Whatever is honorable . . . whatever is lovely, whatever is commendable . . . think about these things" (Phil 4:8). We do well to be wary of finding fault or shortcomings, fixating on what's missing, or saying things like, "I can't believe these people's idea of fun is Sunday afternoon rodeoing" or "It's always cold here." Attitude will impact our ministry; people respond to the signals we give them.

Genuine and Unconditional Love and Acceptance

It can be challenging to love those who are not like us. Again, Christ is our role model: "As the Father has loved me, so have I loved you. . . . Greater love has no one than this, that someone lay down his life for his friends" (John 15:9, 13). One way we can give our lives is to die for those we serve; another is to live for them. When Roxy and I moved to rural Nebraska, the stark differences were eased by a deep love God gave us for the people. This love carried us through our ministry there.

Proverbs 14:31 says that when we treat people with contempt, we show contempt toward their Maker. Instead, we should ask God to help us have a love that accepts people as they are, with Christ once again being our standard: "Accept one another . . . just as Christ accepted you" (Rom 15:7 NIV).

A Willingness to Give Up

First Corinthians 8 and 9 impacted me early on as I navigated from city to rural. Paul writes about foregoing meat offered to idols and even becoming a vegetarian if necessary to reach people cross-culturally. He gave up his right to a kosher diet. He gave up having a wife, family, and regular income, all for the sake of reaching people cross-culturally.

It is interesting how prominent food is in this text. Food alone can be a bridge or a barrier. Our neighbors may cook differently. For us, examples included wild game, raw milk, and some unrecognized dishes. When we say, "Where he leads, I'll follow," we may also need to say, "What they feed, I'll swallow." Besides food, we may give up having people around who are on the same wavelength as ours, extended family close by, familiar amenities like Starbucks and Target stores, or the higher income of a secular job.

Food. Family. Finances. Three *F*'s—it sounds like we need to give the ministry a failing grade. Early on, I wondered. But time in ministry validated for Paul, and has validated for Roxy and me, and will likely someday validate for you (if it hasn't already) that the sacrifices are worth it because of the outcomes. Back to Paul: "I do it all for the sake of the gospel, that I may share with them in its blessings" (1 Cor 9:23). *The sacrifices we make for reaching others cross-culturally with the gospel are the forerunners to blessings.*

Many of these blessings are temporal.[5] We didn't have a world-class restaurant nearby, but we had a great small-town café with home-cooked meals. If you've never been to a small-town church potluck, you haven't lived. People in our church became like family to us. They filled our freezer with meat and our car with garden produce. But these pale in comparison to the eternal blessings of seeing people come to Christ and their lives changed.

I am inspired by Christy, who worked in extremely rural conditions in the Appalachian mountains. A conversation with a local man reveals why she had a fruitful cross-cultural ministry. He said, "I can't believe how much you've sacrificed to come here." Christy replied, "After you've been here a while, the blessings outweigh the sacrifices."[6]

A Willingness to Adapt

One's new culture is unlikely to adapt to us; we must adapt to it. Being set in our ways is not a recipe for an enduring, effective, and joy-filled ministry. Christ again is our example: he "emptied himself" and took on human form in all ways except sin (Phil 2:6–8). Imagine how much he had to adapt! Paul writes,

> To the Jews I *became* as a Jew, in order to win Jews. To those under the law I *became* as one under the law . . . that I might win those under the law. To those outside the law I *became* as one outside the law . . . that I might win those outside the law. To the weak I *became* weak, that I might win the weak. I have *become* all things to all people, that by all means I might save some. (1 Cor 9:20–22; italics added)

5. See Mark 10:28–30, especially the words, "now in this time."

6. I believe I got this quote from the *Christy* television series (1994–1995). The novel *Christy*, a classic by Catherine Marshall, is riveting reading.

If we want to reach a hunter, we do well to become a hunter. If we're going to appeal to more folksy people, then our worship services may need to balance professionalism with participation. There are all sorts of ways to become. Now, we don't need to become in every way; there may be some things that are too uncomfortable. For me, I was willing to work cattle in all ways except castrating bull calves. I had my limits! The more we become, the more people will warm up to us . . . and the more they will be receptive to the gospel we have to share with them.

Teachable

Lingenfelter and Mayers write, "It is noteworthy that God did not come as a fully developed adult; he did not come as an expert. . . . He was an infant, born into a humble family."[7] Even the all-knowing Son of God was willing to enter his new culture as a learner. In Luke 2:46, we find him sitting among teachers, listening, and asking questions. Doing so, "Jesus increased in wisdom and in stature and in favor with God and man" (v. 52). Should we do any less?

There are several ways we can learn. One is through *unconscious imitation*. As we immerse ourselves in a new culture, we'll pick up on things almost without realizing it. Second is *learning about*. We achieve this by reading books, browsing websites, listening to local radio stations, and possibly taking classes.[8] Third is *learning from*. This is done by observing and asking questions. We honor locals when we view them as our teachers.[9]

Caution: Hazards Ahead

Roads have signs that help us avoid hazards. As we navigate through cultural differences, a few road signs are needed.

Caution: Cultural Arrogance

There are two common forms of cultural arrogance. First is *ethnocentrism*—the tendency to judge our new culture by our former culture. In

7. Lingenfelter and Mayers, *Ministering Cross-Culturally*, 16.
8. One good source for rural ministry learning: www.tactprogram.org.
9. Luzbetak, *Church and Cultures*, 188–89.

doing so, we are prone to treat people as backward, primitive, uneducated, unclean, and ill-mannered. We can easily project "I am better than you," or "I am here to improve things." Even if some of our new culture truly is inferior, that does not excuse an air of superiority. Duane Elmer, a believer who has spoken in more than seventy-five countries and provided cross-cultural training for Fortune 500 companies, writes about the predominant response to his question, "What could missionaries do to more effectively minister the gospel of Christ in your culture?" The answer: "Not think they are so superior to us."[10]

The second form of cultural arrogance is *paternalism*—a misguided compassion toward a "lesser" culture. It's treating people like helpless children, implying that they cannot take care of themselves. It makes people more dependent on us.[11]

We can rid ourselves of cultural arrogance by recognizing that our own culture is far from perfect, by adopting a humble approach, by being intentional about finding the good in our new culture, and by temporarily suspending judgment. In time, we may well find that some of their ways of doing things make sense and are perhaps even better.

Caution: Confusing Culture with Christianity

It is easy for us to allow culture to influence our biblical understanding and Christian practices unduly. For example, we might import worship forms from our previous culture without giving much consideration to our new culture. We might impose decision-making forms that are foreign to our rural culture—perhaps more top-down or structured.

Caution: Impatience

It takes patience to learn a new culture and live with people different from us. If our culture values punctuality, it takes patience when people are habitually late. If our culture is perfectionistic, it takes patience to be around more laid-back people. If our culture values getting things done, it takes patience to be with people whose higher value is relationships.

10. Elmer, *Cross-Cultural Servanthood*, 15.

11. Luzbetak, *Church and Cultures*, 65–66.

The greatest need for patience among ministers of the gospel may well be in effecting changes in the culture. We dare not barge in and immediately preach about all that needs to change. In our new culture, we will likely encounter widely accepted practices that are morally abhorrent to us. This requires balance: if we try to bring change too quickly, our ministry may be aborted; if we are too slow to encourage change, we may compromise God's word. It took years for missionaries William Carey to eliminate widow burning and Marilyn Laszlo to stop her tribe's people from burying alive those who had become unconscious.

Perhaps this, in part, is what Paul means when he says, "To the weak, I became weak." We must remember that we all come to Christ as we are, and from there, we slowly become who Christ wants us to be. In New Testament times, certain aspects deeply ingrained in the culture were permitted to continue for a period—such as forms of temple worship, specific Sabbath observances, circumcision, food restrictions, and limiting evangelism to the Jewish people.

At times, the alternative to removing sin is worse. Foreign missionaries have long wrestled with this regarding polygamy. The husband who puts away all wives except one can create problems. How will the other wives and children be cared for? They may resort to prostitution to survive. What will their attitude toward the gospel be if their husbands leave them? Some missionaries have refused to baptize men who had several wives, while they baptized the wives because they had just one husband. The result was a church made up mostly of women.

Wisdom is needed to know when to be patient and when to be a change agent. Sometimes, we need to be like the prophets of old, boldly addressing the sins in our culture. We must be cautious of cultural relativism. We need to be culturally sensitive but not culturally driven. A key prayer is for wisdom to discern what things we need to change and what are not immediate priorities.

Caution: Culture Shock

As we navigate through the early days in our new community, we shouldn't be surprised by disoriented and troubled thinking, uneasiness, irritability, homesickness, a desire to withdraw, anxiety, nervousness, depression, lethargy, boredom, and loneliness. We may experience physical issues, such as headaches and upset stomachs. We may feel like children who must start all over with learning the basics of life, like how to work, eat, talk, and play. These things are normal. In time, they will pass.

If culture shock occurs, there are straightforward ways to address it. It helps to recognize it for what it is. It happens. It's survivable. It doesn't mean we shouldn't be there. It helps to seek God's help through prayer, adapt as much as possible to new cultural norms, make friends, attend local events, boldly try new things, be an explorer, have an adventuresome spirit, and learn all we can about the area.

It helps not to take ourselves too seriously. Someone modified a proverb: "Anything worth doing is worth doing poorly—the first time, and better the second time." In the meantime, we need to be okay when others smile at us—and we need to smile at ourselves. A new rural pastor's wife posted on Facebook: "Tornado sirens going off again, in our bathroom, please pray!" To which a local replied, "That's actually a fire siren, dear!" We must expect things like this during our early days of cultural acclimation.

Most important, when experiencing culture shock, we do well to remember the reason: "I have become all things to all people, that by all means I might save some" (1 Cor 9:22). This is reason enough for perseverance!

Good News: Outsiders Can Become Insiders

It is possible to experience cultural deliverance. You will grow to enjoy your adopted culture and feel at home there. You will achieve cultural competence. There are four typical stages of adjustment.[12] First is the *"How quaint" stage*. It's the honeymoon stage, the stage of initial romance and thrill. It's looking at the culture through the eyes of a tourist.

Second is the *"This just isn't like home" stage*. It's the stage of growing disenchantment. It usually begins in earnest a few weeks after arriving. Expect a recurring longing for the familiar. Expect negative and critical thoughts and feelings. Expect questions like, "Why do they do it this way?" Expect tears and wondering, "Will I ever be happy here?" This stage could last a year or two, with vestiges continuing for several years. Sadly, many move before working through it.

Third is the *"It's starting to make sense" stage*. This is the beginning of cultural resolution, a softening of attitudes. "Back home, we did it this way" is said less frequently. We are now enjoying some of the cultural differences and smiling when those inevitable embarrassing cultural faux pas happen.

12. Klassen and Koessler, *No Little Places*, 66–70.

Fourth is the *"It feels like home" stage*. This is the stage of feeling settled. Frustrations have eased. The worst is over. We may feel like we've gained as much as we've given up. We may even get to the place where we prefer our new culture to our old. It can easily take three to five years before we enter this stage. I knew I had arrived when it felt odd to put on shoes (instead of cowboy boots) when flying to my former home in Phoenix.

Until we are well down the road with these stages, it will be easy to have disparaging thoughts when locals view us as outsiders. But the truth is, that's what we are! It's nobody's fault; it's simply where we begin. We aim to be seen as insiders rather than as foreigners or guests. However, it takes time. When it happens, our family is happy and healthy. More important, the table is set for a thriving church.

Part Three

A Theological Perspective of the Rural Church

7

Can My Small Church Be Healthy?

Rob Beckett

Just as the soundness of a tree is determined by the vitality of its roots, the sustainability and growth of small and rural churches today are deeply intertwined with their health. Drawing inspiration from the Gospel of Luke and Jesus's own words, we will explore how the focus shifts from rapid growth to establishing solid, spiritual foundations; we learn that maintaining church health is not just desirable, but essential. We must shift our gaze from numerical expansion to fostering a spiritually robust and wholesome community. Our faith calls us to cultivate an environment of love, unity, and spiritual nourishment, ensuring that our churches, regardless of size or location, are brimming with life and spiritual vitality.

The book of Acts is a widely utilized Scripture for fostering and explaining church growth. It is frequently referenced and relied upon within the religious community as the standard by which to pattern their strategy and approach to achieving that growth goal. The book of Acts chronicles the explosive beginnings of the church in Jerusalem during Pentecost, when the Holy Spirit descended upon the 120 gathered in Acts 1–2, and through the missions of Paul and Barnabas (Acts 9–28). But we can not only look to the book of Acts for instruction and illustration for the church but also examine the foundations laid out before the growth happened. The church did not suddenly erupt into a freak phenomenon; it happened over time, with Jesus's teaching, walking, talking, and spending life with the disciples, laying the groundwork and foundation for Pentecost to occur. All that happened before the Holy Spirit baptized the newly forming church. So, we must ask, what are the theological basis and spiritual truths established and communicated by our Lord before Pentecost?

Luke authored both the Gospel of Luke and Acts. These two books form a single narrative, from John the Baptist's birth in Luke 1 to the ministry journeys of Paul in Acts 28. Although not as commonly referenced for church growth, the Gospel of Luke lays the foundational ideas supporting the growth in Acts. Luke's Gospel is a prescriptive guide, providing essential principles and teachings. At the same time, the book of Acts takes on a descriptive role, vividly illustrating the unfolding of early Christianity and the power of the Holy Spirit. Together, these two texts form a cohesive narrative that enriches our understanding of the early church and its expansion. Much like the tree David talked about in Ps 1 that was planted by the waters and grew and prospered, the Gospel of Luke delves into the underlying reasons behind events in the early church. In his Gospel account, Luke provides a deeper understanding of the principles that guided the actions and teachings of Jesus and the early disciples.

On the other hand, the book of Acts sheds light on the actual occurrences and practices within the early Christian community. It offers a narrative account of the spread of Christianity, the missionary journeys of the apostles, and the establishment of churches in different regions. Together, these two texts provide a comprehensive perspective on both the theological foundations and the practical aspects of the early church.

Church Health vs. Church Growth

A substantial body of literature has been dedicated to church growth. In previous works, the main objective has been to offer practical guidelines and recommendations for effectively managing and fostering church growth. These resources focused primarily on specific actions and practices required to grow a church successfully. In contrast to this approach, our unique focus lies on church health. We aim to delve deeper and identify the essential qualities and attributes a church must possess to experience growth and achieve sustained success in its mission and impact. By shifting the focus to church health, we believe we can provide a more comprehensive and holistic understanding of what indeed contributes to the long-term flourishing of a church community.

Church growth and church health are intertwined yet have distinct focuses. Regarding growth, we must be attuned to organizing, communicating, motivating, and maintaining control. But when it comes to health, we must embrace a deeper awareness of the spiritual dynamics at play—the essence of service, holiness, outreach, and worship. It's a delicate balance, reminiscing on the past while pondering the present and envisioning the future. By heeding the prescriptive guidance of Luke's Gospel and exemplifying the descriptive practices found in Acts, we can foster a vibrant church that is both fruitful and enduring.

We must remember that our aim goes beyond merely getting bigger; it is to be spiritually alive and engaged with God and his people. This requires harnessing our spiritual gifts, deepening our knowledge of the Bible, being prayerful and generous in our outreach, becoming unified as a body, and living out our faith boldly. As we strive to strengthen the health of our church communities, may we never forget that these efforts are not in vain, for it is through them that the kingdom of God will truly expand. May we also take heart from this truth: the Lord's promise to build and grow his church will always remain true. He is faithful, and he will surely do it!

The questions remain: Can our small rural church be healthy? Can it grow to make a significant impact on the kingdom? The answer is a resounding YES! We must never underestimate the power of God's Spirit and his ability to work through us. As we focus on cultivating church health, let us remember that growth will naturally follow as a byproduct of our faithfulness and obedience to God. We must strive toward building healthy churches that will continue to thrive for generations to come, bringing glory and honor to our faithful God. So be encouraged and stirred toward this goal: to build healthy churches genuinely impacting the world for Christ's sake, one life at a time.

Churches are at their best when they wholeheartedly serve God spiritually. This involves not only the outward expressions of worship and service but also the inward transformation of hearts and minds. When a church is spiritually healthy, it reflects the love, grace, and truth of God to the world.

Defining Health

While there are various ways to measure church health from an organizational standpoint, such as attendance numbers or financial stability, spiritual qualities are the only measure that truly holds significance in God's eyes. These include a genuine love for God and others, a passion for prayer and studying the Scriptures, a commitment to living out Jesus's teachings, and unity in fellowship.

When Jesus spoke to churches and individual Christians, he urged us to prioritize seeking God's kingdom and righteousness. He reminded us that it is through this pursuit that we can experience true fulfillment and an abundant life. When a church aligns itself with God's purposes and seeks to honor him, it becomes a beacon of hope and light in the community.

By focusing on spiritual maturity and discipleship, the local church can thrive spiritually as part of the body of Christ. As believers come together to worship, pray, and learn from one another, they become a unified force for good in the world. They can extend God's love and grace to those in need, and in doing so, make a lasting impact in their communities.

In this way, the spiritual health of a church is not only a matter of personal faith and growth, but it also has a ripple effect extending beyond the church walls. When church members are spiritually vibrant and passionate, the church can inspire others to seek a deeper relationship with God. It can bring hope to the weary, healing to the broken, and reconciliation to the divided.

A Healthy Church Is Governed by Scripture and the Work of the Holy Spirit

Indeed, when a church is rooted in the timeless truth of God's word and guided by the Holy Spirit, things fall into place. The church becomes a place of refuge, a source of encouragement, and a catalyst for transformation. It serves as a reminder that God is at work in the world and that his kingdom is advancing through his people.

The Gospel of Luke presents several insightful spiritual principles that remain relevant to church health lessons today. We must take to heart Jesus's teachings on prayer, obedience, faithfulness, and discipleship. In chapter 11, Jesus focused on the church and the leaders of his day—the synagogue and the Pharisees. Jesus had some powerful words to say to them, and they were not very appreciative of those words. So strong and abrasive were

Jesus's words that one of the leaders spoke up and said, "Teacher, in saying these things, you insult us also" (11:45). However, Jesus was not inflicting insults; he was awakening them to the reality of their spiritual condition.

Jesus's charges against them pointed to and exposed a sick, unhealthy community of faith. The community was being accused of being corrupt from within (v. 39), being completely blind to its faults (v. 40), wasting time and effort on small and trivial things (v. 42), being spiritually dead (v. 44), being rule-bound (v. 46), being hypocritical (vv. 47–51), and suppressing personal growth (v. 52).

As we read through the Gospel of Luke, it is evident that Jesus's primary concern was for people to have the right relationship with God and for the church to live out this truth in love toward one another. In chapter 12, Jesus reminded his disciples to prioritize the fear of God over the fear of man and to trust in God's provision and care for them. He also emphasized the importance of being faithful stewards of all God has given them and being ready for his return.

Jesus's teachings are just as relevant for the church today as they were when Jesus first spoke them. The Gospel of Luke challenges us to evaluate our spiritual health and to realign ourselves with God's purposes. It encourages us to focus on things that truly matter in life, such as loving God and loving others, rather than getting caught up in meaningless pursuits.

To determine whether our small rural church can be healthy, we turn to some critical spiritual principles developed by Jesus in Luke 10–12.

Characteristics of a Healthy Church

The church's health is characterized more by the quality of its spiritual life than the quantity of its worldly success (Luke 11:28, 35–36, 42; 12:22–34).

A healthy church discerns and submits to God's will (11:28, 35–36) while prioritizing spiritual growth and nurturing discipleship (12:22–34). Instead of being preoccupied with external appearances or superficial rules, a healthy church cultivates a heart aligned with God's desires (11:42).

One tendency in seeking success is to reduce everything to the measurable, the immediate, and the right now. So many easily get caught up in the temporal realities of budgets, attendance, and buildings, and forget the fundamental, spiritual battles that threaten the church. But Jesus reminds us that the healthy church fully surrenders to God and seeks his kingdom above all else (12:31–34).

Another tendency to pursue success is prioritizing the means rather than the ends. We can become preoccupied with methods and programs for church growth, losing sight of the fundamental spiritual questions: Why do we desire growth? What are we striving for? Who is the source of our growth? However, Jesus reminds us that a healthy church seeks to obey God and faithfully follows his guidance in all things.

One common inclination in pursuing success is to gravitate toward the dramatic and ostentatious. It's easy to get caught up in marketing and promoting the church, inadvertently neglecting the deeper calling from God to engage in ordinary acts of service and cultivate quiet holiness in our everyday lives.

Jesus serves as a gentle reminder that a truly vibrant church embodies humility, selflessly serving others with love and authentically sharing the transformative message of the gospel through both our actions and our words.

The essence of a healthy church lies not in what it strives for but in what it anticipates (Luke 10:38–42; 11:5–10; 12:35–38).

Our society greatly values constant activity and motion. It is often assumed that a busy church is a thriving church. However, Jesus invites us to embrace a calm and expectant posture, responding to God's will rather than trying to predict it. In Luke 10:38–42, Jesus contrasts the busyness of Martha with the attentive and receptive nature of Mary. It is not by our efforts and striving that the church will thrive, but by humbly waiting upon and responding to God's leading. There is grace in the waiting.

In Luke 11:5–10, Jesus urges us to persist in prayer, trusting in God's faithfulness rather than our strength. Our prayers are not a mere ritual but a genuine conversation with our Heavenly Father, who cares deeply for us and our concerns. Jesus's parable of the persistent friend at midnight highlights the importance of tenacity in prayer, urging us to approach God with boldness and persist in seeking his guidance, provision, and wisdom. This continual asking, seeking, and knocking indicates an attitude of trust in God's goodness and faithfulness. It reinforces our ongoing dependence on him, keeping us conscious of the fact that our strength and success as a church are not self-generated but God-given.

Similarly, in Luke 12:35–38, he instructs his followers to be ready and watchful for his return, living out our faith daily in anticipation of the ultimate fulfillment of God's kingdom. Living in anticipation of God's kingdom does not mean adopting a passive stance, but instead maintaining a dynamic and active faith that continually seeks to embody God's love and justice. As we anticipate the return of Christ, we are called to be attentive to the needs around us, express compassion, uphold justice, and exhibit the transformative power of the gospel in our everyday actions. Stewardship of God's gifts, service to our neighbors and communities, and commitment to living according to God's principles become our daily act of worship. The defining characteristics of a healthy church include a church that is deeply rooted in Christ's love, actively engaged in God's work, and constantly growing in spiritual maturity while awaiting the Lord's return.

A healthy church is defined not by its programs but by the power and clarity of its message (Luke 11:23; 12:8–9).

In Luke 12:8–9, Jesus redirected the church's focus toward its primary mission of proclamation: "And I tell you, everyone who acknowledges me before men, the Son of Man also will acknowledge before the angels of God, but the one who denies me before men will be denied before the angels of God." Remember the importance of boldly proclaiming our faith in both word and deed.

The primary function of any church, regardless of its size, is to proclaim the gospel. The gospel must permeate everything done in the church; if it does not, it fights against the message of Jesus Christ. Gospel proclamation must occupy every aspect of the church's activities. Every program and activity should align with this purpose clearly and directly (11:23). It is essential to recognize that the church is not merely a social or charitable organization; it is the embodiment of Christ's message. While the church does engage in social and charitable initiatives, these serve as vehicles to share the message of grace and forgiveness through Jesus with others. As we eagerly anticipate the second coming of Christ, let us prioritize the proclamation of his message above all else. That defines a healthy and thriving church—one that boldly proclaims the gospel and transforms lives for his glory. Let us continually remind ourselves and each other to focus on surrendering to God's will.

A healthy and vibrant church is defined by its competence and unwavering confidence (Luke 11:11–13; 12:32).

As churches experience growth, they naturally place increased importance on training and skill development. A greater emphasis is placed on selecting competent individuals and putting them in suitable positions, ensuring that experienced and accomplished experts guide the church's performance.

Jesus intentionally chose core leaders who were not conventionally "competent." Peter, a Galilean fisherman with limited eloquence, delivered a powerful sermon on Pentecost that deeply moved the people of Jerusalem. Even more intriguing was Jesus's selection of Judas, who would ultimately betray him. What prompted Jesus to choose these "incompetent" individuals as his allies? John 2:23–25 provides insight: "Now when he was in Jerusalem at the Passover Feast, many believed in his name when they saw the signs that he was doing. But Jesus on his part did not entrust himself to them, because he knew all people and needed no one to bear witness about man, for he himself knew what was in man."

Matthew Henry reflected on this passage, highlighting Jesus's profound understanding of humanity:

> Jesus not only knew people superficially, recognizing their names and faces like we often do, but He truly comprehended their nature, dispositions, affections, and intentions in a way that surpasses our limited understanding. While we may only observe the actions of individuals, Christ possesses a deep knowledge of their innermost being.[1]

Jesus directed his focus toward the incredible potential God had in store for his people. In Luke 11:11–13, Jesus emphasized God's eagerness to bestow "good gifts" upon his children when they ask, seek, and knock. Furthermore, in Luke 12:32, Jesus reiterated God's joyful intention to grant his children the kingdom.

A healthy church is unwavering in its trust in God's provision. While God indeed employs talented individuals, his ability to work through a church hinges not only on their skills or competence but also on the faith they possess. It is vital to remember that God's primary aim is to reveal himself rather than to showcase the abilities of his spiritual children.

1. Henry, *Matthew Henry's Commentary*, 1517.

The hallmark of a healthy church lies not in its decision-making abilities but in its ability to discern with wisdom and insight (Luke 12:54–57).

We often assess a church based on the wisdom and timeliness of its decisions. The building committee decided it was time to repave the parking lot and create some additional spaces in the process. The personnel committee is applauded for its astute management of a recently implemented staff insurance program. The budget committee found a few line-item expenses that could be trimmed to save some money. We are sensitive to the results of the decisions made in a church.

The church's ability to discern is often overlooked—its power to identify spiritual challenges and establish spiritual priorities. In Luke 12:56–57, Jesus clearly articulated the church's primary need to discern: "You hypocrites! You know how to interpret the appearance of earth and sky, but why do you not know how to interpret the present time? And why do you not judge for yourselves what is right?"

The term *interpret* used in this passage originates from the Greek word *dokimazo*, which often refers to assaying metal or thoroughly examining something to determine its suitability for approval.[2] Specifically, Jesus appears to be urging the church to distinguish between actions and intentions that align with God's will and those that do not.

A healthy, vibrant church is distinguished not by its popularity among people but by its unwavering commitment to godly principles of holiness (Luke 11:43; 12:49–53).

The success of a church is often measured by the size of its attendance at programs. The temptation can be to focus solely on developing more activities to appeal to different segments of the congregation, as a growing church is typically seen as effective. However, it's important to remember that true success lies not just in numbers but in the genuine spiritual growth and connection fostered within the church community. In numerous churches, the prevailing assumption is that quantity equals quality—more space, more people, more budget, and more programs. In Luke 12:49–53, however, Jesus addressed the inherent conflict between God's priorities and human popularity: "I came to cast fire on the earth, and would that it were already kindled! I have a baptism to be baptized with, and how great is my

2. Grundmann, "δόκιμος."

distress until it is accomplished! Do you think that I have come to give peace on earth? No, I tell you, but rather division."

The church today is called upon to prioritize God's holiness. In a true sense, the church takes a stand against the worldly system. Unfortunately, the church often focuses solely on delivering a message of love and forgiveness, neglecting its responsibility to address the world's sinful and hostile rebellion against God. Let us strive for a more balanced approach, acknowledging the call to love and the urgency to confront the world's rebellion. In Rom 1:18–32, Paul spoke of the battle line between the church and the world: "For the wrath of God is revealed from heaven against all ungodliness and unrighteousness of men, who by their unrighteousness suppress the truth."

In today's world, a healthy church must be defined by what it stands for and against. It should wholeheartedly advocate for holiness, sacrifice, and justice, even in the face of increasing hostility toward such principles. Pursuing popularity and acceptance will undermine the church's effectiveness in carrying out God's work.

A thriving church is distinguished not by the amount of its wealth but by the integrity of its intentions.

Numerous churches demonstrate a distinct preoccupation with money—acquiring and allocating it. Frequently, church initiatives for the year are closely tied to projected revenues. We are advised that prudent management necessitates a fiscally conservative approach for churches. Luke 12 contains a rather lengthy discourse concerning Jesus's view of money. "And he said to them, 'Take care, and be on your guard against all covetousness, for one's life does not consist in the abundance of his possessions'" (v. 15). "Instead, seek his kingdom, and these things will be added to you" (v. 31). "For where your treasure is, there will your heart be also" (v. 34).

Sometimes, the church can become overly focused on financial matters, perhaps to the detriment of its time and energy. Don't get me wrong; the church must handle money responsibly. But we tend to put a lot of emphasis on committees like the finance/budget committee. In many churches, this committee plays a dual role as the program committee, making decisions about the church's program agenda.

A thriving church recognizes the spiritual significance of financial matters. Let us not make budget decisions merely based on practicality but seek spiritual discernment. Our budgets should align with our spiritual priorities. Moreover, when facing financial challenges, let us embark on a prayerful journey to uncover spiritual and fiscal causes. Together, we can overcome and rise above all obstacles!

The healthy church understands the profound impact of its financial practices on the world's perception of it. When a church accumulates debt that exceeds its capacity to repay, it inadvertently conveys to the broader community a message of irresponsibility and a lack of control within the Christian community. Similarly, when a church allocates 90 percent of its budget to internal operations, it unintentionally conveys a message of limited vision and faith within the Christian community. The church must recognize the long-term implications of its financial decisions and strive to display wisdom, stewardship, and a deep commitment to its mission.

Churches are truly at their healthiest when they wholeheartedly serve God in a spiritual sense. While various organizational measures exist to gauge church health, the spiritual aspects hold the most significance to God. Remember, Jesus spoke not only to churches but also to individual Christians, urging us to prioritize seeking God's kingdom and righteousness above all else. By doing so, the local church will flourish spiritually as part of the body of Christ, and everything else will fall into place. It's a beautiful reminder of the timeless wisdom that continues to resonate today.

Conclusion

Even a small church can radiate robust health and spiritual vitality if it embraces and embodies the principles laid out above. It's not the size of the congregation that determines church health but rather the degree to which its members live out the gospel in their daily lives. A small church that values holiness, practices self-sacrifice, seeks justice, and manages its resources wisely can have a profound impact on its community. Influence is not measured by size but by the integrity of the intentions and the authenticity of its love. As members of such a church seek first God's kingdom and righteousness, they will invariably witness the hand of God at work, transforming their small congregation into a beacon of hope and a testament to the powerful truth that health and growth in the church are ultimately the work of God's Spirit. Remember, church health is not about the numbers—it's about the heart!

As we examined the book of Acts, we uncovered a narrative of the early church's growth and expansion. Acts is descriptive, painting an illustrative picture of how the early believers lived out the teachings of Jesus and how God blessed their faithfulness with exponential growth. Yet, the growth model of Acts is incomplete without the foundational teachings of Jesus in Luke, which provide the formula for church health.

In Acts, we see a vibrant and thriving community of believers who embodied the teachings of Jesus, shared their possessions, and gathered regularly for fellowship and prayer. Their unity, love, and devotion to the teachings of Jesus were the fertile soil in which exponential growth took root. In Acts 2:47, we read, "And the Lord added to their number day by day those who were being saved." Notably, the expansion was not the result of clever marketing strategies or ambitious expansion plans but a natural outcome of the church's health and vitality.

However, the growth in Acts should not be viewed in isolation from the teachings of Jesus in Luke. The principles of holiness, sacrifice, justice, and prudent financial management that Jesus laid out in Luke 10–12 form the bedrock upon which the church's health and growth must be founded. Without this foundation, the growth described in Acts becomes unsustainable and short-lived.

Acts illustrates the growth model of the church, but Jesus's teachings in Luke provide the necessary blueprint for church health and growth. A church founded on the principles outlined in Luke and living them out, as seen in Acts, will invariably experience health and growth. When this happens, the church is now aligned with God's purposes and empowered by his Spirit. Let's embrace this truth and strive to become the church God intends us to be, regardless of our size or location.

8

Is There Hope for Our Dying Church?

Kyle Bueermann

Picture this scene with me for a moment: it's Sunday morning, thirty minutes or so before the start of the weekly worship gathering. A pastor of a small, rural congregation finds himself alone in his office, but he knows he can't stay there. Soon, he'll have to go into the sanctuary and see the folks who've gathered that morning. His office window faces the parking lot, so he can already tell it won't take long to greet the folks who showed up.

He already knows the questions he'll be asked: "Pastor, where is everybody this morning?" He can also predict some of the not-so-subtle verbal jabs that will come: "It seems like there are fewer people here *most* weeks, pastor." "We drove past the church down the street, and *their* parking lot is full this morning."

A couple of families have already left for that "other" church. "We like their music." "They have more to offer for our kids." And now another family wants to set up a meeting later in the week to talk. He has a pretty good idea they'll be on their way out soon, too. That probably means an already tight budget year will look even bleaker.

As the pastor prepares to leave his office, he takes one last look over his sermon notes but secretly wonders if anyone gathered that morning cares what he—or the Bible—has to say. He secretly wonders what value his master of divinity degree would have in the marketplace. Before shutting his door, he asks, "Is there any hope for our little church?"

Maybe this story reminds you of a pastor you know. Perhaps that pastor is you. Week in and week out, you labor in the work of the ministry—visiting the sick, praying for the discouraged, meeting needs here and there, having gospel conversations when the opportunities arise, and preparing biblically faithful sermons. Then, sometimes, you step back and look around, and it seems like nothing at the church is improving for all that effort.

Folks don't seem to care about the gospel. Their lives don't look more like Jesus. Sometimes, the longer they attend your church, the *worse* their lives look! Marriages are failing, and folks continue to struggle with addictions. On top of that, the air conditioner in the sanctuary isn't cooling like it should, and the roof leaks more and more each time it rains. Can you relate? In such times, you may wonder if God has a plan for your church.

If you've been there before or are there right now, take heart! This chapter is for you. So, read on and see how our God loves to do amazing things among dead and dying churches!

Is It Biblical for a Church to Die?

In his book *Reclaiming Glory*, Mark Clifton, senior director of Replant for the North American Mission Board of the Southern Baptist Convention, asks, "What about a dying church brings glory to God?"[1]

In Rev 2 and 3, we see Jesus threatening to kill a couple of churches. On second thought, that may be a bit too harsh. He warns that he will "come to you and remove your lampstand from its place" (Rev 2:5). The image of the lampstand represents the presence of Jesus in his church. In other words, while the body may continue to meet as a religious or social club, it would cease to be a New Testament church of the Lord Jesus Christ.

What would cause Jesus to make such a serious threat? Sin had crept into the body of some of the churches, and they refused to repent. Here is what we see from these churches in Revelation:

- In Ephesus (Rev 2:1–7), they had forgotten their first love. They had a lot of good things going for them, but they allowed something else to take the place of Jesus in the life of their church. In short, they were idolaters.

1. Clifton *Reclaiming Glory*, 11.

- In Pergamum (Rev 2:12–17), they failed to keep a close watch on their doctrine, and false teachers came in and took over.
- In Sardis (Rev 3:1–6), the church had numerous activities going on and appeared healthy from the outside, but Jesus says they were actually dead on the inside.
- In Laodicea (Rev 3:14–22), they had become lukewarm. They were just going through the motions of ministry, but there was no passion there whatsoever.

In each of these cases, the call is the same: repent, turn around, and rediscover what it means to worship Jesus. If the church does not heed this call, it will cease to exist as a church.

In a sense, we can say that, yes, it is biblical for a church to die. But that's only if the church refuses to repent of how they got off track and return to their first love, Jesus Christ. If your church is pursuing Jesus (and that starts with a pastor pursuing Jesus), then I would say emphatically, "No! It is not biblical for your church to die."

The God of New Life

The Bible is full of stories of God bringing dead and dying people back to life. In one of the most well-known miracles from Jesus's ministry, he raises Lazarus back to life after he'd been dead for three days (John 11:1–44). One of the most remarkable accounts in the Bible of God bringing life and hope where there were only death and destruction is found in Ezek 37, and it's that passage to which we'll turn our attention for most of this chapter.

> The hand of the Lord was upon me, and he brought me out in the Spirit of the Lord and set me down in the middle of the valley; it was full of bones. And he led me around among them, and behold, there were very many on the surface of the valley, and behold, they were very dry. And he said to me, "Son of man, can these bones live?" And I answered, "O Lord God, you know." Then he said to me, "Prophesy over these bones, and say to them, O dry bones, hear the word of the Lord. Thus says the Lord God to these bones: Behold, I will cause breath to enter you, and you shall live. And I will lay sinews upon you, and will cause flesh to come upon you, and cover you with skin, and put breath in you, and you shall live, and you shall know that I am the Lord." So I prophesied as I was commanded. And as I prophesied, there was a sound, and

> behold, a rattling, and the bones came together, bone to its bone. And I looked, and behold, there were sinews on them, and flesh had come upon them, and skin had covered them. But there was no breath in them. Then he said to me, "Prophesy to the breath; prophesy, son of man, and say to the breath, thus says the Lord God: Come from the four winds, O breath, and breathe on these slain, that they may live." So I prophesied as he commanded me, and the breath came into them, and they lived and stood on their feet, an exceedingly great army.
>
> Then he said to me, "Son of man, these bones are the whole house of Israel. Behold, they say, 'Our bones are dried up, and our hope is lost; we are indeed cut off.' Therefore, prophesy, and say to them, thus says the Lord God: Behold, I will open your graves and raise you from your graves, O my people. And I will bring you into the land of Israel. And you shall know that I am the Lord, when I open your graves, and raise you from your graves, O my people. And I will put my Spirit within you, and you shall live, and I will place you in your own land. Then you shall know that I am the Lord; I have spoken, and I will do it, declares the Lord." (Ezek 37:1–14 ESV)

At the beginning of this passage, Ezekiel faced a bleak situation. We're told the hand of the Lord leads Ezekiel to the middle of the valley and that it is full of bones. Not only that, but they were "very dry," meaning there hadn't been any life in that valley for a very long time. And it was unthinkable that life could be restored to that valley. Lamar Cooper puts it plainly: "Any suggestion that there could ever again be life in the bones would appear preposterous."[2]

Charles Spurgeon gives an even clearer picture:

> These bones could by no means raise themselves. We never heard of such a thing as a dead man restoring himself to life, though he be but newly buried, if he be indeed dead: he cannot lift a hand towards his own reviving. These bones were without a trace of life. The flesh was gone, devoured by kites and jackals, or rotted and scattered in impalpable powder to the four winds of heaven. How could these carcasses raise themselves? There was no trace of moisture left upon them; they could not give themselves life or motion; it was a fool's hope to look for such a thing.[3]

2. Cooper, *Ezekiel*, 323.

3. Spurgeon, "Despair Denounced," 471.

The only thing Ezekiel could see around him was death and destruction. At the same time, everywhere he looked were reminders of what once was. We are told later that these bones become a vast army. So, helmets, spears, shields, and armor would be spread across the valley along with the bones. At one time, this was a mighty fighting force, but now, all Ezekiel could see would be a painful reminder of how things *used* to be.

Perhaps you can relate. It could be that every Sunday when you walk through the halls of your church building, you're reminded of what once was:

- Classrooms that *were once* filled with lively discussions.
- A nursery that *used* to rattle with the sounds of children playing.
- A choir loft where spectacular musicals *were once* produced.
- Many empty pews or chairs where people *once sat.*
- A baptistry that *was once* active regularly.

Sometimes, it might even be depressing to walk through your building and see all the reminders of what *used* to be. I have served in churches with a sanctuary that seats several hundred, with a gathered congregation of only a few dozen. In those instances, it's obvious every Sunday that the church is a far cry from what it once was.

In verse 3, God asks Ezekiel the key question of the passage: "Can these bones live?" If we are honest, the answer to this question is obvious. The bodies that once housed all these bones have been dead for a long time. From the description we are given, all the flesh has rotted away. There's nothing left of the bodies but bones. So, of course, the natural response to God's question is, "Of course not! There's no hope for these bones whatsoever!"

You might even be tempted to answer that way when someone asks you if there's hope for your church. "There's no hope here. These people don't care about their community. They don't care about sharing the gospel with their coworkers. They don't even really care about what I'm preaching; they only care that I show up every week since they're paying me."

Thankfully, Ezekiel understands with whom he is speaking, and he's not about to tell God no! So, he has a much more diplomatic answer: "Oh Lord God, you know." Ezekiel knew he could not tell God no, but he also knew that nothing short of a miraculous work of God would bring any hope to the valley.

At this moment, Ezekiel realized he was powerless to carry out the task before him. No book or ministry event could bring life to this valley.

No, if the bones were going to live again, they did not need a program or a pep talk; they needed a miracle.

The same is true in the work of ministry. As you look out at your congregation each Sunday, you may wonder how the next video study or Sunday school curriculum can infuse new life into these folks. Let me be clear: there's nothing wrong with a new book study or curriculum. These are fantastic tools available to us. But none of them has the power to revive your folks. That power belongs to the Holy Spirit and the Holy Spirit alone.

For a dying or declining church to experience revival, it must experience a true movement of God. No other answer is sufficient. No program in the world can spark a revival.

In response to Ezekiel's answer, God issues a command: "Prophesy over these bones." On the surface, this command seems irrational, doesn't it? Here, Ezekiel is in the middle of this valley, surrounded by nothing but old weapons, armor, and many dry bones. God commands him to preach! And here's the message: "Oh dry bones, hear the word of the LORD!"

I've often wondered what Ezekiel was thinking at this moment. He's in the valley all alone. He's looking at the bones around him, and the Lord has just commanded him to preach. If he were like me, he'd think, "This is ridiculous. There's no real hope here. I'm just wasting my time when I could be doing other, more important things with my life."

Have you ever felt that way? Perhaps you stand before your people each week, preaching sermon after sermon, and never see any change in them. At times, maybe you even feel like you'd be better off preaching to dry bones. Have you ever wondered if you were just wasting your time?

But God's message for the bones (and for Ezekiel) doesn't stop there. God tells them exactly what he's about to do. Look again at verses 5–6.

> I will cause breath to enter you, and you shall live. And I will lay sinews upon you, and will cause flesh to come upon you, and cover you with skin, and put breath in you, and you shall live, and you shall know that I am the LORD.

A lot happens in these two sentences, but notice where the emphasis lies. Ezekiel's job is to declare the message God has given, and in response, God will do the work of bringing the bones back to life. That's good news. You and I cannot bring dead and dying churches back to life. Revitalizing and replanting is primarily spiritual (hence, Jesus's call on the churches in Revelation to repent).

Of course, a lot of work must still take place. A pastor cannot simply sit in his office for forty hours a week and expect the church to grow, for church growth is not merely a pragmatic process. A four-step checklist or a silver-bullet approach guaranteeing success does not exist. But if the Spirit of God works, even the most bleak-looking church can experience extraordinary life and growth once again.

In verses 7–10, we see Ezekiel's obedience to this very unusual command from God. Ezekiel preaches to the bones: "So I prophesied as I had been commanded" (v. 7). So, Ezekiel has a choice. Will he trust what God has told him, even in ridiculous circumstances? Will he have the faith to do the eccentric?

Several pastors reading this can relate to Ezekiel's dilemma. If we're honest, some Sundays, you've stood in the pulpit, and it felt like you were preaching to nothing but dry bones. Maybe you've even wondered if you were crazy to stand there week after week and proclaim the word of the Lord to a room of people who look and act as if they'd rather be elsewhere.

But, as soon as Ezekiel begins to prophesy—as soon as he is obedient to the task the Lord has given him—something starts to happen. Bones come together. Tendons appear. Flesh grows. Skin covers them.

For the first time in years, it looks like there's life in the valley. God moved through the preaching of his word! Have you seen that happen? Even in places where you weren't sure God could still move, he softens hearts, and stuff starts happening. New life begins to emerge where there was only bickering and anger before.

If you were to stumble upon the valley of dry bones at this point, you'd think it was an impressive army. But something significant was still missing.

Where there were once only dry bones, it now appears there's an army in this valley. Something has changed dramatically. And yet, at the same time, something is missing. The end of verse 8 simply says, "But there was no breath in them." Should an enemy show up to fight at this moment, this seemingly impressive-looking army would be completely defenseless. They looked good, but there was no breath in them. They had no life.

In Rev 3:1, Jesus says to the church at Sardis: "I know your works. You have the reputation of being alive, but you are dead" (ESV). The church at Sardis looked alive. I imagine this meant they had a lot of ministry activities happening. They were very busy. Maybe they even drew a crowd when they gathered each week. But, to use Ezekiel's words, there was no breath in them.

Don't miss this, pastor. This is a hard truth. Your church might look healthy and vibrant, but have no life whatsoever. You might be busy with church events and committee meetings each week. But all this activity can be completely devoid of the Holy Spirit. Warren Wiersbe said, "Too often God's people are like that standing army, lifelike but not alive."[4]

"Wait a minute!" you might be thinking. "Jesus said if two or three are gathered in his name, he's there among them!" Yes, he did. You are correct. However, the caveat is that those gathered are gathered in the name of Jesus. It is possible to gather—even as a church—under something other than Jesus's name. You can gather simply in the name of your church. You can gather in the name of your church's denomination. You can gather in the name of your preferred worship style or even in the name of "We're not your average church." However, the only thing that brings real life into a church is the Spirit.

As you read over this passage, look at where the emphasis for the action lies. God says repeatedly, "I will." The work of ministry is fundamentally spiritual. We can't manufacture it. The Holy Spirit must move for change to occur. But how often do we rely on our strength to accomplish what can only be achieved through the work of the Holy Spirit?

How many Sundays have you considered your rural church and thought about everything you *can't* do? How often have you wondered if there is hope for this small, struggling church? If you have, I urge you to cling to this passage as a lifeline.

It is not your job to revitalize the church. It is not your job to grow the church. It is not your job to save souls. It is your job to "shepherd the flock of God that is among you, exercising oversight, not under compulsion, but willingly, as God would have you; not for shameful gain, but eagerly; not domineering over those in your charge, but being examples to the flock" (1 Pet 5:2–3). It is your job to "preach the word; be ready in season and out of season; reprove, rebuke, and exhort, with complete patience and teaching" (2 Tim 4:2). Then, trust as you do so, God will do what only he can do: bring new life.

For the people of Israel, they thought all hope was gone: "Our bones are dried up, and our hope is lost; we are indeed cut off" (Ezek 37:11). Maybe you've felt like this as you labor for the sake of the gospel at a small church in a small town where it seems like nothing significant can happen.

4. Wiersbe, *Wiersbe Bible Commentary*, 1331.

But oh, my friend, don't lose heart. God can do amazing things in the smallest and most out-of-the-way places. Why? Because of what he tells Ezekiel in verses 13 and 14: "Then you will know that I am the Lord." God loves to use small places to accomplish big things, so we can't simply say, "Look at what that church has done," or "Look how much that pastor has accomplished."

God loves to work in such a way that, when others see it, they say, "Look what the Lord has done here." No other explanation for the new life coming to the valley of dry bones could explain what God had done. Where there had once been only death and decay, now a mighty army of the Lord was standing ready for service.

The same is true of churches. Where there once were only reminders of what *used* to be, the Lord can do work and bring new life to a church. Where there once was a building no one in the community paid attention to, the Lord can restore a place of ministry and vitality for an entire town.

The End (or the Beginning) of the Matter

God can do it! He's done it before, and he can do it again in your church in your community. Richard Blackaby said, "God is under no obligation to resource your plans for his church, but he will spare no expense under heaven to resource *his* plans for his church."[5]

Your job is not to figure out what you want to do and then try and get God to bless it. That would be like Ezekiel setting out to stitch each bone in that valley together to create an army. Your job is to follow Christ and his plan for his church: preach the word, love the people, and serve the community.

Just as sure as God raised the dry bones in the valley back to life, he can bring new life and new hope to churches in the smallest of communities. Will you follow him? Will you lead your church to trust and obey him?

So, pastor, as you step into the pulpit this week, rest in this truth. God is at work. God can accomplish his purposes. Remember that God is at work in your church this Sunday, regardless of how many cars are or aren't in the parking lot, and regardless of how full the sanctuary may (or may not) be. Rest in the assurance that God is at work as you print the bulletin, as you plan the music and teach Sunday School, as you listen to an angry church member's complaint for the tenth time, and as you do any number

5. Richard has made this statement at several conferences hosted by the North American Mission Board Replant Team.

of other things in your weekly routine. As you do, trust that God is working in ways you may not see or even understand for days, weeks, or even years to come.

And pray that when all is said and done, this will be the testimony of your church and community: "Then you will know that I am the LORD. I have spoken, and I will do it. This is the declaration of the LORD" (Ezek 37:14).

9

Defining Success in Rural Ministry

Martin Giese

Every man and woman serving Christ in rural contexts has pondered the implications of the question, "How do we define success in rural ministry?" However, before considering the answer to that question, we must be alert to the possibility of a flawed assumption. In defining success in rural ministry, the danger is that we can assume our task involves embracing our current cultural definitions of success and somehow adapting those metrics to the realities, limitations, and constraints of rural ministry.

Instead, our task involves replacing cultural definitions of success with biblical definitions of success. The question then becomes, "How does God define success in ministry as outlined in his word?" and "What are the implications of that theological understanding for those of us who serve in rural ministry leadership?"

In this chapter, we begin with an overview of examples from the Old and New Testaments in which God corrects his servant's misconceptions of success (what success is not) in ministry and affirms his definition of success. We need to replace culturally based metrics with theologically based metrics for measuring success. This theological reset of our definitions of success will enable us to replace anxiety over "results" with contentment and hope, resting in the preeminence of Christ and his evaluation of our ministry in rural places.

What Success Is Not: A Brief Overview of Some of the Misconceptions of Success from Biblical History

Lessons on Success in the Old Testament

Success is not achieving a goal through spiritual compromise and/or disobedience, regardless of the vision's grand and/or compelling nature.

Early inhabitants of the Shinar plain had an ambitious and compelling vision—the kind of vision our twenty-first-century culture would have embraced. They said to each other, "Come, let us build ourselves a city and a tower with its top in the heavens, and let us make a name for ourselves, lest we be dispersed over the face of the whole earth" (Gen 11:4). It was a breathtaking prospect. Who would not want to be part of a highly visible, history-changing achievement? The problem, of course, was that the ambitious and compelling vision was an act of direct disobedience to a divine commission given to Adam and Eve and their descendants: "Be fruitful and multiply and fill the earth and subdue it" (Gen 1:28) and reiterated to Noah (Gen 9:7). The "Shinarites" were well on their way to success by their definition when God vetoed the vision, confused the languages, and dispersed mankind.

Many generations later, King Saul edited a specific command from God and followed the popular course for monarchs of his day. He set aside God's directive to destroy a wicked nation utterly and instead preserved the material wealth of that nation for his national temporal gain. He then attempted to justify his disobedience under the guise of sacrificial commitment. God responded through the prophet Samuel: "Has the Lord as great delight in burnt offerings and sacrifices, as in obeying the voice of the Lord? Behold, to obey is better than sacrifice" (1 Sam 15:22). Saul's apparent royal success was, in fact, a spiritual failure. Saul forfeited his position as king (1 Sam 15:26).

It even happened to a "man after God's own heart." King David of Israel, caught up in pride and self-sufficiency, initiated a census of his fighting men. Few things are as intoxicating to the ego as a large following. The tally was impressive. However, God's reaction was severe judgment (1 Chr 21). David had slipped into a common leadership sin of trusting and taking pride in his resources rather than relying upon the Lord.

Ministry success requires obedience to God. God's parameter for measuring success is always confined to the sphere of obedience to his word, his ways, and his example. The affirmation of that truth echoes throughout all the Hebrew Scriptures of the Old Testament.

God admonished Joshua, "This Book of the Law shall not depart from your mouth, but you shall meditate on it day and night, so that you may be careful to do according to all that is written in it" (Josh 1:8).

King David charged his successor to the throne, "Be strong, and show yourself a man, and keep the charge of the Lord your God, walking in his ways and keeping his statutes, his commandments, his rules, and his testimonies, as it is written in the Law of Moses" (1 Kgs 2:2–3).

King Hezekiah's epitaph affirms the same truth: "For he held fast to the Lord. He did not depart from following him but kept the commandments that the Lord commanded Moses" (2 Kgs 18:6). "Thus Hezekiah did throughout all of Judah, and he did what was good and right and faithful before the Lord his God" (2 Chr 31:20).

By God's measurement, true success is not measured by the size of the vision, the experience of the action, or the array of resources. Instead, God simply asks, "Did you obey me?" Ministry success is always measured within the sphere of spiritual obedience.

Success is not necessarily defined by or achieved through expediency—seizing a moment, an opportunity, a contextual advantage, or being first to the most and the best.

With ambition and selfishness, Lot chose the Jordan Valley, including the fertile plains bordering Sodom and Gomorrah, for his location and livelihood (see Gen 13:11). Abraham was left with the most difficult and dismal context for making a living.

We, however, know the rest of the story. Lot's legacy is of continued compromise, moral corruption, and spiritual failure. Abraham is honored in the word of God as the father of the faithful. Our conception of seizing an opportunity may not be God's conception. Again, obedience to God takes precedence over timing on the road to ministry success. Throughout the Hebrew Scriptures, success is defined by fidelity to God and obedience to his word.

Lessons on Success in the New Testament

That pattern is also evident in the New Testament references to spiritual/ministry success. God's measurement of success is modeled and explained by Jesus and further defined by the clear teaching of New Testament Scripture.

Success Is Measured by Self-Sacrifice and Service

Jesus modeled and taught that success is measured by eternal investment:

> Do not lay up for yourselves treasures on earth, where moth and rust destroy and where thieves break in and steal, but lay up for yourselves treasures in heaven, where neither moth nor rust destroys and where thieves do not break in and steal. For where your treasure is, there your heart will be also. (Matt 6:19–21)

Jesus modeled and taught that spiritual success is not self-preservation but self-sacrifice.

> If anyone would come after me, let him deny himself and take up his cross and follow me. For whoever would save his life will lose it, but whoever loses his life for my sake will find it. For what will it profit a man if he gains the whole world and forfeits his soul? (Matt 16:24–26)

Jesus modeled and taught that spiritual success is not about attaining a position where others serve you, but rather about embracing a posture of service to others.

> But whoever would be great among you must be your servant, and whoever would be first among you must be your slave, even as the Son of Man came not to be served but to serve, and to give his life as a ransom for many. (Matt 20:26–28)

Success Is Completing God's Assignment

Spiritual success is not reliably measured in the quantity of our investment of time, energy, and money but rather in completing the work God has assigned to us. Christ affirms his success when he states, "I glorified you on earth, having accomplished the work that you gave me to do" (John 17:3–4).

Following Pentecost, the example of the early church reflected spiritual/ministry success measured by acts of devotion and obedience that were fundamentally relational, not programmatic. "And they devoted themselves to the apostles' teaching and the fellowship, to the breaking of bread and the prayers" (Acts 2:42).

Success Is Measured by Relationships Rather than Numbers

While the Old Testament presents warnings about placing confidence in numbers of people as a focus of trust and pride, the whole of Scripture, especially the New Testament, gives surprisingly little place to numbers in measuring success as it relates to ministry.

Two references specifically highlight the number of believers in the growth of the early church. Both references came in response to the sermons delivered by Peter. In Acts 2:41 and 4:4, we read, "So those who received his word were baptized, and there were added that day about three thousand souls" (2:41), and, "But many of those who had heard the word believed, and the number of the men came to about five thousand" (4:4).

The consistent focus of New Testament teaching measures spiritual success relationally, not numerically. It points to growth in understanding and obedience to the word of God. It aims to deepen our relationship with God and with one another. References to numerical growth, when they appear, are not attributed to ministry technique, vision, or strategy but instead to God's work among his people

> And they devoted themselves to the apostles' teaching and the fellowship, to the breaking of bread and the prayers. And awe came upon every soul, and many wonders and signs were being done through the apostles . . . praising God and having favor with all the people. And the Lord added to their number day by day those who were being saved. (Acts 2:42–47)

Note the consistency of the emphasis upon relational metrics of success in the commendations of the apostle Paul to the churches in his Epistles:

- To the church at Ephesus: "For this reason, because I have heard of your faith in the Lord Jesus and your love toward all the saints, I do not cease to give thanks for you, remembering you in my prayers" (Eph 1:15–16).

- To the church at Philippi: "I thank my God in all my remembrance of you, always in every prayer of mine for you all, making my prayer with joy, because of your partnership in the gospel from the first day until now. . . . And it is my prayer that your love may abound more and more, with knowledge and all discernment" (Phil 1:3–9).
- To the Colossians: "We always thank God, the Father of our Lord Jesus Christ, when we pray for you, since we heard of your faith in Christ Jesus and of the love that you have for all the saints" (Col 1:3–4).
- To the Thessalonians: "We give thanks to God always for all of you . . . remembering before our God and Father your work of faith and labor of love and steadfastness of hope in our Lord Jesus Christ" (1 Thess 1:2–3). "We ought always to give thanks to God for you, brothers, as is right, because your faith is growing abundantly, and the love of every one of you for one another is increasing" (2 Thess 1:3).
- To Philemon: "I thank my God always when I remember you in my prayers because I hear of your love and of the faith that you have toward the Lord Jesus and for all the saints" (Phlm 4–5).

Jesus commends the churches of Revelation on a similar basis. The commendations that are given do not mention church size, church membership numbers, or numerical growth.

He writes:

- To the church at Ephesus: "I know your works, your toil, and your patient endurance, and how you cannot bear with those who are evil but have tested those who call themselves apostles and are not, and found them to be false. I know you are enduring patiently and bearing up for my name's sake, and you have not grown weary" (Rev 2:2–3).
- To the church at Pergamum: "I know where you dwell, where Satan's throne is. Yet you hold fast my name, and you did not deny my faith" (Rev 2:13).
- To the church at Thyatira: "I know your works, your love and faith and service and patient endurance, and that your latter works exceed the first" (Rev 2:19).
- To the church in Philadelphia: "'I know your works. Behold, I have set before you an open door, which no one can shut. I know that you have but little power, and yet you have kept my word and have not denied my name" (Rev 3:8).

The Importance of Context in Measuring Success

To measure success, we must understand our setting. Every ministry context is unique. There may be parallels, but no duplicates. A significant difference exists between succeeding where it's easy—think fertile soil—and succeeding where it is difficult—amidst rocks, weeds, and resistance.

Contextual awareness is essential but often overlooked in our efforts to measure success, leading to inadequate and inaccurate assessments. That is one reason why numeric measurements are not a reliable measure of success. Numeric measurements fail to reflect context. Numeric measurements may reflect results and outcomes, but they do not indicate the task's difficulty, the strength of the opposition, or the presence or absence of favorable or unfavorable circumstances. For example, the record of the conquest of Canaan by the nation of Israel includes a variety of contexts and results unrelated to numerical superiority or numerical measurement. Consider the following summary of some of the locations and outcomes of conquest for the nation of Israel:

- Jericho: Success via miraculous intervention. The walls of Jericho fell outward.
- Ai: Failure because of individual disobedience. Achan kept some spoils of war.
- Gibeon: Failure due to national deception and a lack of seeking God's wisdom.
- Jerusalem: Victory through perseverance and divine intervention.
- Southern and northern Canaan: Success through obedience and God's blessing.
- Following the conquest, the occupation of the promised land by Israel involved some partial successes and some failures.
- Yet the people of Manasseh could not take possession of those cities, but the Canaanites persisted in dwelling in that land. Now, when the people of Israel grew strong, they put the Canaanites to forced labor but did not utterly drive them out (Josh 17:12–13).

The historical record of the nation of Israel from Judges through Malachi includes cycles of success and failure directly tied to the degree to which Israel and its leaders obeyed God.

The teaching and examples of ministry in the New Testament also reveal that not all contexts are created equal. Some contexts are significantly more difficult than others. Some contexts are considerably less difficult than others.

Jesus's explanation of the parable of the sower contrasts four separate outcomes of the sowing of the same seed.

> Hear then the parable of the sower: When anyone hears the word of the kingdom and does not understand it, the evil one comes and snatches away what has been sown in his heart. This is what was sown along the path. As for what was sown on rocky ground, this is the one who hears the word and immediately receives it with joy, yet he has no root in himself, but endures for a while. When tribulation or persecution arises on account of the word, immediately he falls away. As for what was sown among thorns, this is the one who hears the word, but the cares of the world and the deceitfulness of riches choke the word, and it proves unfruitful. As for what was sown on good soil, this is the one who hears the word and understands it. He indeed bears fruit and yields, in one case a hundredfold, in another sixty, and in another thirty. (Matt 13:18–23)

In another passage, Jesus denounces the spiritual resistance of three communities—Chorazin, Bethsaida, and Capernaum—as greater than that of Tyre, Sidon, and even Sodom!

> Then he began to denounce the cities where most of his mighty works had been done because they did not repent. "Woe to you, Chorazin! Woe to you, Bethsaida! For if the mighty works done in you had been done in Tyre and Sidon, they would have repented long ago in sackcloth and ashes. But I tell you, it will be more bearable on the day of judgment for Tyre and Sidon than for you. And you, Capernaum, will you be exalted to heaven? You will be brought down to Hades. For if the mighty works done in you had been done in Sodom, it would have remained until this day. But I tell you that it will be more tolerable on the day of judgment for the land of Sodom than for you." (Matt 11:20–24)

Similarly, in the expansion of the New Testament church, as described in the book of Acts, responses to the gospel and the ministries of the apostles varied widely. In some contexts, the response to the preaching of the gospel was very positive—many believed:

- "Now many signs and wonders were regularly done among the people by the hands of the apostles. And they were all together in Solomon's Portico. None of the rest dared join them, but the people held them in high esteem. And more than ever, believers were added to the Lord, multitudes of both men and women" (Acts 5:12–14).
- Joppa: "Then, calling the saints and widows, he presented her alive. And it became known throughout all Joppa, and many believed in the Lord" (Acts 9:41–42).
- Berea: "Now these Jews were more noble than those in Thessalonica; they received the word with all eagerness, examining the Scriptures daily to see if these things were so. Many of them therefore believed, with not a few Greek women of high standing as well as men" (Acts 17:11–12).
- Corinth, where the synagogue ruler and many citizens believed: "Crispus, the ruler of the synagogue, believed in the Lord, together with his entire household. And many of the Corinthians hearing Paul believed and were baptized" (Acts 18:8).

In some contexts, the response to the preaching of the same gospel was very negative. Great opposition occurred.

- In Lystra, Paul was stoned and left for dead: "But Jews came from Antioch and Iconium, and having persuaded the crowds, they stoned Paul and dragged him out of the city, supposing that he was dead" (Acts 14:19).

In many contexts, the response to the preaching of the gospel was mixed.

- In Antioch in Pisidia (Acts 13), some Jews and converts to Judaism were open to the gospel (vv. 42–43). Yet many Jews were hostile and jealous of the crowds (v. 45). Many gentiles believed (v. 48). The Jews incited people of influence, and the apostles were driven out of town (v. 50).
- At Philippi (Acts 16)—Lydia was converted (v. 15). A fortune teller's accusations led to the beating and imprisonment of Paul and Silas (vv. 19–24). And the Philippian jailor was converted (v. 34).
- In Thessalonica: "And some of them were persuaded and joined Paul and Silas, as did a great many of the devout Greeks and not a few of the

leading women. But the Jews were jealous, and taking some wicked men of the rabble, they formed a mob, set the city in an uproar, and attacked the house of Jason, seeking to bring them out to the crowd" (Acts 17:4–5).

- In Ephesus (Acts 19), the responses included both revival and riot.
- In Rome, Paul was imprisoned but allowed to preach. Paul "lived there two whole years at his own expense, and welcomed all who came to him, proclaiming the kingdom of God and teaching about the Lord Jesus Christ with all boldness and without hindrance" (Acts 28:30–31).
- While in Athens, the audience was intrigued, but the response was mixed. "Now, when they heard of the resurrection of the dead, some mocked. But others said, 'We will hear you again about this.' So Paul went out from their midst. But some men joined him and believed, among whom also were Dionysius the Areopagite and a woman named Damaris, and others with them" (Acts 17:32–34).

What is evident on the pages of Scripture is sometimes forgotten in the trenches of rural church ministry. Context matters! In twenty-first-century rural ministry, some pastors are serving in communities like Berea. Some pastors are serving in communities like Chorazin, Bethsaida, and Capernaum. Some churches are attempting to reach communities like Lystra. Some are trying to reach communities like Corinth or Ephesus.

The metrics of success in Berea were highly visible. The metrics of success in Philippi are less obvious and more varied.

Failure to recognize the vast differences in the ministry context leads to unwarranted boasts of success and premature laments of failure. It also results in unbiblical comparisons and unhelpful advice to ministry leaders.

Having been part of dozens of ministry leadership events throughout North America over several decades, I have been exposed to radically differing concepts of ministry success. I have left some events with the impression that the key to ministry success was to find a high-growth suburb within a rapidly growing city and ride the tsunami of population transfer to ministry stardom. Conversely, I have left some events with the notion that true ministry success is only measured in a continual repetition of activities that have been passed down to us without heed to any measurable effect or change. Neither extreme has biblical support.

Furthermore, the word of God more frequently frames ministry success in terms of how God-followers respond to their respective contexts rather than how they influence or alter them. Rejoicing in suffering, being patient in trials, and persevering through difficulty resulted in God bringing about outcomes that altered contexts and glorified him. As Paul points out, "I planted, Apollos watered, but God gave the growth. So neither he who plants nor he who waters is anything, but only God who gives the growth" (1 Cor 3:6–7).

Defining Success in Rural Ministry: Rediscovering an "Old" Metric

Numbers are unreliable, ministry contexts are infinitely varied, and ministry results are challenging to quantify and measure. So, how are we to gauge success in rural ministry? And can we really measure success at all?

I say yes to the question, "Can we measure success?" To do so, we need to replace our cultural metrics for measuring success with biblical metrics. This requires us to consider a fresh approach to how (and what) we measure.

In the Hebrew Scriptures, the word translated "success" is closely related to both the subjective and objective conceptions of "a good outcome"—the desired outcome at the inception of an endeavor. Here, too, a significant relational component of the concept exists. A good outcome is measured subjectively by the hopes and desires of the person(s) involved. Spiritual success, in this sense, could be thought of as the outcome that God desires.

In the Greek language of the New Testament, there are no words that translate directly to the English word and concept of "success." This does not mean God is apathetic toward outcomes for his church. Yet, it does show us that God is not as preoccupied as we frequently are with the notion that a particular goal must have a specific, measurable, and/or numeric outcome.

Further, the dichotomy of "success is all about numbers" and "success is all about repetition of techniques, approaches, and methods of ministry" (often defined as faithfulness) needs to be set aside. Success is not "all about numbers." Nor is success all about the repetition of efforts that have little or no desired outcomes.

In defining and measuring ministry success, our fidelity is to a Person, not a program, an eternal ministry, not a temporal method. Many methods of ministry that bear fruit in a context for a time have an effective "shelf life." That is, they may not remain effective or bear fruit as the context changes and new generations appear. The word of God affirms both faithfulness and fruitfulness. We are called to be faithful. We are appointed to be fruitful. "Moreover, it is required of stewards that they be found faithful" (1 Cor 4:2 ESV). "If you abide in me, and my words abide in you, ask whatever you wish, and it will be done for you. By this my Father is glorified, that you bear much fruit and so prove to be my disciples" (John 15:7–8).

A Biblical Measurement of Success

Success is better defined for all churches and ministries (including rural ministries) in terms of process—movement toward a destination that God desires—rather than arrival at a specific point that we desire, mark, or measure.

Within Scripture, we see multiple categories of success. We are succeeding when:

- The proclamation of the gospel continues and expands through us in our context (Acts 5:28, 42; 8:4; 20:20–21).
- The understanding of the gospel is increasing among those we serve and those with whom we serve (Acts 19:20; Col 1:3–14; 2:6–7).
- The people we serve are developing the biblical characteristics of identifying disciples of Jesus in the Bible; for example, the fruit of the Spirit (Gal 5:22–23) and the characteristics of spiritual maturity (Eph 4:13–16; 2 Pet 1:5–8).
- The people we serve respond biblically to the varying realities of their individual and corporate contexts (Gal 5:18–24; Phil 1:9–11; 4:4–9).
- The aforementioned processes continue in the presence of difficulty or opposition. We persevere (2 Cor 4:7–10; 11:23–28; Phil 3:7–17; 1 Thess 1:2–3; 2 Thess 1:4; Heb 12:1–2; Jas 1:12).
- The processes mentioned above are not limited to the repetition of the familiar (sometimes confused with faithfulness) but are subject to creative modification aimed at greater effectiveness (allowing for fruitfulness). We are concerned with both faithfulness and fruitfulness. As a result, we are willing to set aside a method of ministry if it no longer contributes to the fruitfulness of that ministry (1 Cor 4:2; 9:19–23; Rev 2:10, 19; Matt 3:8; John 15:5, 8).

In specific contexts, faithfulness to biblical principles will yield visible results and measurable outcomes. There will be an increase in the number of people we serve. People will receive the word with gladness. The church and its influence for Christ will expand. Celebrate those moments and give glory to God, who gave the increase!

In some contexts (often in rural contexts), fruit will result and be "exported." Disciples will be produced and will move away to other fields of service. The ministry will expand, but the number of people in your location may not. Celebrate the contribution to the kingdom!

In other contexts, faithfulness and fidelity to the gospel message and its ministry may cause frustration and opposition within the mission field. Perseverance will be required, but may not be visibly rewarded on this side of eternity. God has honored you by entrusting you with an assignment of great difficulty! Take heart that you are historically aligned with a company of the faithful, highly honored and celebrated in heaven (Heb 11)! And keep your focus on Jesus!

> Let us run with endurance the race that is set before us, looking to Jesus, the founder and perfecter of our faith, who for the joy that was set before him endured the cross, despising the shame, and is seated at the right hand of the throne of God. (Heb 12:1–2)

Conclusion

Defining success in rural ministry (and all ministries) involves replacing sociocultural metrics with biblical metrics. The process is as important as the product.

The teaching of the word of God provides parameters. Ministry success cannot be achieved through spiritual disobedience or temporal expediency. The legitimacy of the spiritual means determines the legitimacy of the spiritual ends. Ministry success requires obedience to God, eternal investment, and sacrificial service.

Ministry success is not reliably measured in total work accomplished or the size of the investment of time, energy, and money, but rather in discerning and completing the work God has assigned to us.

The example of the early church reflected spiritual/ministry success measured by acts of devotion and obedience that were fundamentally relational, not programmatic. Relationships with God and with fellow believers dominate the biblical records of both achievement and commendation.

Understanding ministry context is vitally important in evaluating and measuring ministry success. Similar ministry investments in diverse ministry contexts may yield vastly different ministry outcomes. Context often renders numerical measurement of ministry success unreliable. We must give attention to both faithfulness and fruitfulness in our ministry investments.

We must keep an eternal focus on outcomes. When numbers increase and positive results are measurable, give glory to God. When you export your "fruit" to other parts of the kingdom, celebrate the kingdom's impact. When fidelity to mission and ministry results in opposition, focus on Jesus!

> But one thing I do: Forgetting what is behind and straining toward what is ahead, I press on toward the goal to win the prize for which God has called me heavenward in Christ Jesus. All of us who are mature should take such a view of things (Phil 3:13–15).

Part Four

A Theological Perspective of the Rural Pastor

10

Will the Real Church Leaders Please Stand Up?

Understanding the Role of the Rural Pastor

TJ Freeman

"We must save the church! The grocery store is closing, the hardware's gone dark, and the postmaster is worried about consolidation. That church building is all we have left!"

Those words, spoken by a frustrated small-town businessman, reflect the decline affecting many rural communities. Although his concerns are about the preservation of bricks and mortar, he is right to be worried about the shuttering of the small-town church. Abandoned churches are not uncommon scenery on a drive through rural America. A few years ago, a little white church near my house collapsed into a pile of rubble and remains untouched. It appears the only people who would have cared are buried across the street! This trend will likely continue as more churches are left behind by congregations that can no longer sustain them.

Many factors contribute to the decline of the rural church. Perhaps the most significant is the decline in the population of rural communities. This trend disrupts social order, often leading to the crumbling of a wholesome-looking facade that once adorned small-town life. As social pressure to be active in the community wanes, small towns begin to take on the individualistic emphasis of broader society. Stalwart institutions, like the Grange (an agricultural advocacy group started after the Civil War), the town choir, and many civic organizations, have disbanded for lack of interest. Small-town churches may be one of the last institutions to succumb to the shift away from compulsory civic involvement, but they are not exempt. The expectation that upstanding citizens will participate in the church's life has largely vanished, leaving pews, plates, and leadership positions unfilled.

Leadership problems are particularly prevalent and dangerous in small-town churches. I often open my inbox and find multiple requests from people in pastorless churches asking if I can recommend a pastoral candidate or send pulpit supply. Others seek direction, noting an alarming trend that will result in an empty church if something doesn't change. Some of these churches have been without healthy leadership for years! Often, the last "successful" pastor was a one-hit wonder who failed to train young men to replace him. A church without a shepherd is prone to discouragement and desperation. The number of rural churches with empty pulpits exceeds the pool of men entering the ministry, exacerbating the problem.

The empty pulpit, or the fear of it, leads many congregations to make bad leadership decisions. Poorly defined leadership structures, the empowerment of unqualified leaders, domineering church members, and the proliferation of unhealthy leaders have weakened the church. As churches dwindle, these problems, which may have only been masked in leaner years, are magnified.

Sadly, church leadership is often one of the last issues declining churches address. For leadership, it is often easier to imagine that the problem lies in something more superficial or at least entirely out of their control. The church would grow if it only had a more contemporary worship style, more programs for children, a nicer building, or a more spiritually minded community.

Due to their longevity, rural congregations often filter reality through a romanticized understanding of their past. They remember the glory days when the pews were full, children huddled around flannelgraphs, and the choir director had to make cuts for the Christmas cantata. They reason that if they could return to their previous ways, they might achieve historic results. These expectations are sometimes fueled by a domineering individual or family who leverages their influence to become a de facto church leader. Unhelpful leaders have stunted many rural churches on a crusade to return or cling to past practices.

Additionally, some rural churches are hindered by unhelpful structural constraints due to their longevity. Often, outdated bylaws—more common with prohibition-era business models than those of the New Testament church—exist in churches today. Cumbersome congregational statutes may prescribe leadership offices absent from Scripture, such as a board of trustees or leadership by committee. Others may insist upon arbitrary criteria such as a minimum number of elders or deacons. Churches bound by documents such as these are forced to make poor leadership decisions, which often go unaddressed. This is especially problematic in a season of church decline.

Even if a church recognizes the need to address leadership issues, it must navigate an endless sea of promising but deceptive solutions offered by the gurus of our day. Most notoriously, the CEO model, popular in various forms for over a century, entices those who have seen the "proven success" of strong leadership in other churches. While this model has achieved visible results, few compare it to the kind of leadership modeled in the New Testament. Numbers never tell the whole story and are not held out by God as the standard of success. They may even mask the truth or stand as a hollow substitute for faithfulness.

Churches often empower men who can play to the crowd or scratch itching ears. Many of these men worry more about building a platform than remaining faithful. Churches without a pastor for a long time are especially vulnerable to installing self-centered pastors. During a season of exasperation or desperation, their earnest desires may yield to "warm body syndrome" as they empower anyone willing to stand in the pulpit. Installing any of these leaders may provide short-term relief but ultimately lead to long-term regret.

The Bible is not silent about the kind of leadership God intends for his people. Both Testaments provide imagery to instruct God's people regarding leadership. Namely, the people of God are to be led by a plurality of qualified men whose leadership is anchored in serving as a shepherd. The shepherd motif plays on repeat in the pages of Scripture, teaching God's flock to identify men who demonstrate the heart of a shepherd as their leaders. Rural churches, even in decline, must resist the temptation to submit to any other form of leadership.

Shepherding Is a Risky Business

As crucial as shepherd leadership is, shepherds and their flocks should consider the many dangers to shepherd leadership. Stern warnings are issued throughout Scripture to impress upon the hearts of the leaders the importance of remaining faithful to God's design. Despite these warnings, men have ignored God's instructions for selfish gain. Sad examples from Israel's history are found in the stern words of the Old Testament prophets Ezekiel, Jeremiah, and Nahum as they pronounced God's judgment on the shepherds due to their poor leadership. The sins of negligence, selfishness, abuse, and distracted interests are cited as the source of God's anger against these men. Poor shepherding was a liability in Israel that incited the wrath of God. These warnings must be considered carefully!

The New Testament demonstrates the importance of shepherding according to God's design. James tells us there will be stricter judgment for those who teach (3:1), a responsibility given to all shepherds. Peter reminds us that church leaders are not the ultimate authority but undershepherds who must answer to the chief shepherd (1 Pet 5:1–4). The writer of Hebrews indicates that the shepherds will give an account for the authority they exercised within the flock (13:17). God has been very clear throughout Scripture that his people are to be led by shepherds who care for the flock as men who will give an account to God. This is a dreadful, yet noble, task based on God's design for the church.

The Role of a Shepherd in the Church

A healthy rural church must understand, practice, teach, and defend the principles of church leadership demonstrated in Scripture. Throughout history, God and his people have upheld the shepherd motif as the proper means by which God's flock is to receive oversight and care. A healthy rural church is governed not according to practical wisdom or cultural norms but by the shepherd-leadership God has instituted. Therefore, a church needs to have a clear view of the role of the shepherd.

According to ancient agricultural norms, from which the illustration is taken, a shepherd cares for and oversees a flock of sheep. More certainly, a shepherd gives his life to ensure the health and vitality of the flock entrusted to his care. This is not based on the merit of the sheep but on the purpose for which they exist. The sheep are chosen, cared for, and led so they might bring a return on their owner's investment. The job of the shepherd is to help the sheep fulfill that purpose. This will require him to know and appropriately direct each sheep for the fulfillment of the purpose of the flock.

A good shepherd must identify and respond to the challenges associated with the flock and each of its members. He calls the sheep by name as he counts them. He understands their issues, attends to their needs, and guides them appropriately. Familiar imagery depicting the life of a shepherd might include him leading the flock to food and water, numbering them one by one, searching for missing sheep, protecting them from danger, guiding them along the proper path, and applying loving correction when they stray.

The work of a shepherd often comes at a significant personal cost. A shepherd is expected to risk his very life for the sake of his sheep. Before becoming king of Israel, David served as a humble shepherd. In 1 Sam 17:34–36, David recounts his entanglements with lions and bears in defense of the flock to which he was entrusted. Similar language is used in John 10:1–16 to describe how Jesus, the chief shepherd, laid down his life for his sheep. The work of a shepherd is, by nature, personal and sacrificial.

Leaders must rely on these timeless principles to tend God's sheep in a modern rural church context. No modern equivalents or shortcuts exist for the modern-day rural shepherd. Under the direction of the chief shepherd, pastors must do what God's shepherds have always done. They are to provide care and oversight that arises from the word of God while leading the flock to the intended destination of Christlikeness. Shepherds are required to know, lead, feed, and defend the flock under the authority of the chief shepherd.

Know the Flock

The shepherd-leader knows his flock. He is invested in them because they have been entrusted to him. Knowing his congregation from behind the pulpit is not enough for a pastor. He must know them across the dinner table as well. Personal knowledge of the sheep is vital for the care required to replicate the shepherd motif.

The apostle Peter communicates the importance of knowing the flock with the personal language, "Shepherd the flock of God that is among you" (1 Pet 5:2 ESV). Similarly, Luke instructs church leaders to pay careful attention to the flock of which they have been made overseers (Acts 20:28). These commands imply a personal, intimate knowledge of a specific flock that translates into effective leadership and care.

For the shepherd to be found faithful, he must focus on getting to know and care for his flock on two levels: personally and contextually. As the Scriptures exemplify, a good shepherd will attend to the needs of each sheep. This is vital. Daily pastoral work cannot be neglected without negative consequences for the flock. Remember how God chided the Old Testament shepherds of Israel for neglecting the sheep!

If a rural pastor is to be faithful in these duties, he needs to maintain accurate membership rolls. This allows him to have a clear view of who is in the flock so he can be accountable for their care. It is not enough to say that those who attend the church for a season are considered members of the flock. Nor is it helpful to have a list full of people who have not attended church for a long time. Many rural churches boast of a sizable membership yet have rolls filled with dead men and apostates. The shepherd's job is to know exactly who is in the flock and to count them by name.

Although individual member care is an important priority, a shepherd must divide his time wisely for the good of the entire flock. He must develop the skill of maintaining one eye on each sheep while concentrating his gaze on the care and direction of the flock. For a rural pastor, this means understanding the context of the congregation and the community in which they reside. A shepherd who does not consider the church's history, the congregation's disposition, theological leanings, social nuances, regional influences, and how each member impacts the whole has failed to shepherd the unique flock God has entrusted to him properly. Each church has its unique history, personality, and perspective on reality. The faithful shepherd considers these matters as he leads them from their current state to be more like Christ.

Lead the Flock

Sheep are not known for their ability to lead themselves. Therefore, a shepherd must know his flock and how to lead them. Like the one mentioned in Psalm 23, a good shepherd directs the sheep from where they are to where they need to be by charting the course, setting the pace, and providing the security and sustenance required for the journey. Sometimes, the journey involves navigating especially ominous terrain with sheep. The shepherd's job is not to avoid difficulty but to lead through it wisely and lovingly.

A rural pastor must recognize that leadership is not an optional aspect of his ministry. He must be committed to providing more than just preaching and presence. A shepherd-leader, because he knows the flock, has a sense of what is required to lead them to the destination of Christlikeness. He will uphold a clear vision of what it looks like for a congregation to be faithful to God's word as he drives toward the intended destination. He will discern areas where the flock needs to grow and develop as part of their journey to honor Christ in all areas of life. Most importantly, according to the word of God, he will lovingly and patiently guide the flock as an act of shepherd leadership.

Good shepherding is not only focused on directional leadership but also on daily leadership through more prudential issues. What should a congregation do if they have outgrown their building? What kind of outreach best serves the community? Which ministries should receive the most support? What if members disagree? A wise shepherd-leader does not ignore matters such as these. He does not leave them for the loudest voice or majority to decide. He does not assume it will all work out as he sits in the study with his nose in a book. Instead, he assesses and leads because these daily issues contribute to the flock's health. The unique circumstances in the life of each congregation require careful, humble, and clear leadership from the shepherds God has entrusted to them.

Feed the Flock

Sheep require daily nourishment. A good shepherd ensures that, whether the flock is grazing in a comfortable pasture or navigating rugged terrain, daily food is served. In every season, a shepherd-leader prioritizes the feeding of his flock. In Matt 4:4, Jesus quotes Deut 8 to remind his people that man does not live by bread alone but by every word that proceeds from the mouth of God. God's word is the food rural congregations should expect their shepherds to provide. This requires careful and consistent preparation through study, prayer, and assessment. Adequate preparation allows the pastor to serve the word of God as nourishing food through his preaching, teaching, and counseling.

Many rural churches have died the slow, painful death of spiritual starvation. Others are thin and anemic. Still, others have been spoiled by stuffing themselves with spiritual junk food. It is the responsibility of the faithful shepherd to insist that the congregation maintains a steady diet of nutritious food prepared by the Chief Shepherd. The word of God alone has all the community needs to thrive. It provides everything necessary for spiritual health, and there are no substitutes (2 Tim 3:16–17). Only the word of God is alive and powerful, containing everything we need for life and godliness, and can equip a Christian for every good work (Heb 4:12; 2 Pet 1:3).

Be An Example to the Flock

It should also be noted that rural pastors must not deliver the food in some dry, uninteresting, wooden fashion. Too many rural pastors have thought it their duty merely to declare the word, but this is not the job of a shepherd! A shepherd must be an example to the flock, demonstrating the beauty of God's word as he responds with joy and gratitude in his own life and anticipation in the lives of his flock (1 Pet 5:3). God has spoken, and he will act! His word will not return void. If the shepherd's heart is not moved by this reality, he will do no good to the sheep who have grown weary of the blandness of his food. I have heard from many rural pastors who insist the problem of spiritual decline is the fault of unmotivated church members. He would do well to consider the motivations of his own heart and the dreadful dryness of his lips.

A similar danger exists in the hearts of those who feel they need to add to God's word or force an emotional response. Others have no idea how to see or communicate the argument of Scripture in a way that is faithful to the original intent yet applicable today. The message of God's word is not to be tampered with by the shepherd but delivered with the tone, emphasis, and application God intended when he inspired the text to be written. The rural church needs a great reformation when it comes to the feeding of God's flock. This is a shepherding issue that each rural congregation must address if it is to survive.

A faithful shepherd must make it his habit to feast upon the same food he serves the flock. If the word of God does not richly nourish the pastor's soul, he should not expect to impact the members of his church positively. A malnourished shepherd is weak and unable to provide the care required of a man in his position. The rural pastor must prioritize his nourishment before attempting to feed the sheep.

Defend the Flock

I was almost a decade into my ministry before I fully experienced the responsibilities required to defend the flock. A false teacher crept into the church, initially fooling everyone, including me! In time, it became apparent that the elders would need to take a public stand against this man's divisive schemes. This experience was more difficult than anticipated, but it didn't surprise us. The presence of bad actors in the life of the church has been a familiar aspect of church history. As Paul reminded Timothy, evil opponents and impostors have attempted to cause division in God's flock since the days of Moses (2 Tim 3:8). It is the responsibility of the shepherd-leader to be ready to respond to any attempts to cause harm to God's flock.

A rural pastor will find it unwise to wait until he perceives a threat to prepare for battle. The old cliché that says the best defense is a good offense rings true in the church's life. A faithful rural shepherd-leader establishes the best defense by consistently preaching the word, preserving sound doctrine, and demonstrating faithfulness to God and the flock. This offensive work will pay dividends during difficult times. Knowing, feeding, and leading the flock is critical for the defense of the flock when the occasion arises.

Rural church members are not only in danger from the schemes of false teachers within the church but also from without. No longer are rural communities insulated from the worldly pressures once typical of more cosmopolitan demographics. Today, images, ideas, and influences come over the river and through the woods, twenty-four hours a day, at high speeds on fiber optic strands finer than human hair. The faithful rural pastor is unlike Andy Griffith, who protects Mayberry from children riding bikes on the sidewalk.[1] He is more like a soldier on the front lines of battle, protecting the flock from the enemy's most hideous attacks. The shepherd lulled by his rurality into a false sense of ease or tranquility should expect to see casualties in his ranks. Even the most alert and equipped pastors cannot escape the painful reality of cultural damage to their flock. Still, it is the responsibility of the shepherd-leader to do all he can to defend and protect the sheep.

1. Leonard, *Andy Griffith Show*.

Under the Watch of the Chief Shepherd

I have noted that a shepherd of God's flock carries out his responsibilities under the watchful eye of the Chief Shepherd, Jesus Christ. In 1 Pet 5:4, we are reminded that when the Chief Shepherd appears, he will reward his undershepherds with the unfading crown of glory. We are similarly reminded in Heb 13:17 that church members are required to submit to the elders of the church as men who must give an account. Shepherd leaders must never forget that their service is carried out under the direction and watch of a greater authority. Like a good police officer, a shepherd-leader understands that their position does not serve their own purposes, but rather the good of the people, according to an already specified standard.

The failure of many rural pastors to know, lead, feed, and defend their flock results from their inability to consider the authority of Christ in the church's life. Instead of serving, considering the reality that they will face the Chief Shepherd one day, they are busy trying to survive today. But today is only essential because of tomorrow! A faithful shepherd-leader always has the end in mind, driving him to remain steadfast in his daily duties.

A rural pastor can easily forget how much his church matters in God's economy. After a few years of describing your community as a town "in the middle of nowhere that no one has ever heard of," the lie becomes easy to believe that rural ministry is less significant. A pastor who feels his church is neither seen nor important opens himself to the temptation of lowering the bar in several areas. He may not prepare as hard for a sermon he'll preach to the same twenty people who have attended for years. He may not be as apt to push the congregation theologically. He may not believe his church can have any meaningful impact on the community, region, or the world. He may tolerate an unkempt building, a carelessly created bulletin, or an outdated environment. These temptations must be battled, for God has never established an insignificant church!

On the contrary, God sees each congregation as vitally crucial to his eternal plan to glorify himself to the ends of the earth (Eph 3:10–11)! Rural shepherds would do well to see the strategic importance of their church, which may exist in a place with no other visible representation of the gospel! The world may not consider a small, forgotten community a strategic outpost for advancing Christ's kingdom. A denomination may not be interested in less-populated areas. Few will give any attention to remote regions. How much more important it is for rural shepherds, entrusted with the care of the church in the far reaches of society, to demonstrate the value of Christ's work in the middle of nowhere! In God's economy, every rural church is highly strategic and prized.

Theology Applied

Who should lead the rural church? The right man for the job is willing to devote his life to the role of a shepherd. Yet, the responsibility for shepherding even a small flock is too great for one man. This is why the Old and New Testaments commonly refer to shepherds in the plural. A rural congregation is wise to affirm more than one man to shepherd the flock. These men must be held to the qualifications established in 1 Tim 3:1–7 and Titus 1:6–9. Moreover, the office they fill must be understood as a gift from the Lord to empower each member for valuable service in the body (Eph 4:7–16). A plurality of qualified, member-empowering shepherd-leaders is part of God's design for the health of his church. A healthy rural church will devote itself to prayer for these kinds of leaders. Moreover, they will always be on the lookout for men given by Christ to fill this role, even as they train and equip the next generation for this responsibility (2 Tim 2:2).

The ancient shepherds of Israel and some first-century leaders in the church saw shepherding as a means for shameful gain. Rural pastors must be on guard against the temptation to follow the example of these wayward leaders through the misuse or abuse of their office. The temptation to pursue peace at any cost, to allow the de facto leadership of a domineering person or family, to neglect the souls of each member, or to coast along doing as little as possible are everyday temptations to rural church leaders. A frustrated rural pastor often longs for a flock different from the one entrusted to his care. This kind of thinking demonstrates a self-centered focus not far from the behavior that prompted the cry of Ezekiel against shepherds who were only feeding themselves instead of the flock.

The only hope a rural pastor has for avoiding these errors is to look to Christ! The church belongs to him. He is the head of the body, the bridegroom of the bride, and the Chief Shepherd of the flock. Each rural pastor must confess with the apostle Paul,

> For his sake I have suffered the loss of all things and count them as rubbish, so that I may gain Christ and be found in him, not having a righteousness of my own that comes from the law, but that which comes through faith in Christ, the righteousness from God that depends on faith—that I may know him and the power of his

> resurrection, and may share his sufferings, becoming like him in his death, that by any means possible I may attain the resurrection from the dead. (Phil 3:8–10)

A plethora of books, videos, and conferences promoting competing leadership models can be found. Yet faithful shepherd-leadership must be our model. Many attractive-looking alternatives exist, but no substitutes must be accepted for the practices detailed in Scripture.

A faithful rural pastor must resist the temptation to sacrifice the difficult work of shepherding at the altar of numeric growth or an easier path. His mantra must be faithfulness over fruitfulness, as he relies on Christ to do the work only he can do. The goal of the rural pastor is not to see visible fruit but to faithfully care for God's flock, no matter the results.

Conclusion

Pastoring a rural church may not seem like a strategic move. Declining populations and obscure locations are not appealing to many. Yet, rural churches are critical in God's eternal plan to glorify himself! The gospel must be made visible to the ends of the earth, even in the most uninhabited places. This happens as healthy churches gather, making the manifold wisdom of God visible in a way that transcends a rural community and reaches the rulers and authorities in the heavenly places (Eph 3:10–11). Because they are so essential, these rural outposts should be led by well-qualified, highly gifted men who desire to shepherd the flock of God no matter the cost.

The heart of a rural shepherd should mirror that of the businessman who lamented the shuttering of the small-town church. The church is all we have! Only she does not exist for the sake of a nice facade. The church represents the hope of the world according to the mercy of God! Jesus said in Matt 16 that he is building a church, and the gates of hell will not prevail against it. Christ will not allow the church, even in rural places, to cease. Therefore, rural pastors, as shepherd-leaders, must continue to lead and care for God's people in the middle of nowhere. The stakes are high, the responsibilities are significant, and it is worth it!

11

Is My Ministry Important?

John Hindley

We yearn for importance. We yearn to stand on the platform at a major national conference, ending the perfect talk with the room in stunned silence at the beauty and glory of Christ. Yet this is not our experience. Many of us preach to a few saints in lonely isolation. The message is received politely, but inside, you wonder whether your ministry means anything to the kingdom of God.

We might not necessarily crave the importance of celebrity (well, not openly!), but we want to matter. We want our lives to leave a mark and our ministries to have a legacy. Aside from our proud daydreams, though, we know more deeply that it is what is essential to God that will define whether we are important or not.

We long for this to be the case. We want the gospel to have an impact. We believe preaching God's word to the lost is what the Holy Spirit uses to open blind eyes. Discussing the power of preaching the death and resurrection of Christ, Paul likens it to the same creative power with which God spoke light into existence: "For God, who said, 'Let light shine out of darkness,' has shone in our hearts to give the light of the knowledge of the glory of God in the face of Jesus Christ" (2 Cor 4:6).

We long to see this power at work through our preaching and ministry. We want to see the light shining in new hearts. We want to see the church growing stronger and godlier. We delight to see new life or ongoing growth, but we often see so little, so slowly. We question whether the Lord has really called us to this ministry and whether the Spirit has truly given us the gifts we need to exercise it. We dream of more fruit with less drudgery; maybe we dream of more fruit elsewhere.

To put the question starkly, even if I succeed before Christ in my calling as a rural pastor, does it matter? Is there any importance to this work? Can it be satisfying even if it often doesn't feel like it? Once again, it is in the character of God that we will find our answers; in his divine nature, we can learn to measure importance from the perspective of ages, not simply of days or even of years.

Lack of Importance: The Day of Small Things

Many of us feel our ministry is carried out in the day of small things. In Zech 4, the prophet looks forward to the day when Zerubbabel will complete the rebuilding of the temple in Jerusalem. Through the lens of Zerubbabel, Zechariah sees an image of Christ, who will ultimately build the final temple of living stones to his Father's glory. As part of this prophecy, Zechariah writes, "For whoever has despised the day of small things shall rejoice and shall see the plumb line in the hand of Zerubbabel" (Zech 4:10).

Whether we are meant to despise the day of small things seems ambiguous. What is clear is that we do indeed despise it. We long for more and surely a sense in which we should do so. Christ is building his church, and the Father draws worshippers from all nations to his Son. Our longing is a desire set in our hearts by the Holy Spirit to be a part of this great work.

A Creeping Resentment

The danger in despising the day of small things is that it can easily become a despising of the small things themselves, for some small things are people. Some of the small things might indeed feel as though they are not truly part of our calling; I spent yesterday evening mending a toilet in the bathroom of our church building and swapping out a failed battery in the intruder alarm system we have for the tenants in our offices. On a good day, I enjoy learning new skills and being resourceful, but too often, I resent these chores.

This resentment can then easily spill over into places that are even more sinful. When I got home from the church building, I needed to read carefully through an email from a fellow elder about a sad pastoral situation where a church member had serious doubts about God's love and lacked assurance. I was tired and did not know what to say. I did not resent my brother or the church member struggling, but I had to pray several times for love, gentleness, and faithfulness. I needed to do this because I was tempted to resent the Lord.

Too often, I wish there were more hands to do the work. I tell myself that I would be better able to serve the church family if I were not tightening bolts on toilet seats. I tell myself that if I could devote more time to prayer and the ministry of the word, I would be godlier, and the church would be packed with new believers.

We wish we had more impressive music, better administration, a compelling website, or attractive posters. We long for the gifts we see oozing out of the big churches in the suburbs. Our ministry feels unimportant and discouraging. Yet this is what the Lord has chosen to give us. He must see things differently. If I served the church better without the diverse demands of my time, he could easily remove them. Jesus must have given me what he knows will be the greatest blessing to me and those I seek to serve.

A Different Perspective

Rather than despising the day of small things, maybe we should ask how God sees it and how he views those of us who live through it. Then we might see how we should live in the day of small things.

Rural ministry often feels small and unimportant in the eyes of the world and even the church. Rural pastors can be asked questions like, "Why are you wasting your time, your gifts, or your education in the middle of nowhere?" One response is to seek to escape this insignificance, looking for a bigger, more important ministry elsewhere.

Others are tempted to sideline the ministry in the church, living for another ministry. This might be writing, blogging, or chaplaincy to the local police, fire service, or service in a mission agency. These are good things and can be an excellent complement to church-based ministry. The problem is when they become our focus and a diversion from our calling to this small church in this small place. It may not be another ministry. We might pour our energies and hearts into a second job, the improvement of our town (or home), or a hobby. Again, these are good things that can be done to the glory of Christ. But not if they supplant our calling to the church.

So, how do we live in the day of small things if we are resolved not to escape or ignore them? The Lord connects the day of small things with the day of glory. He will bring this great day about by grace (Zech 4:7), not by might nor by power, but by his Spirit (4:6). This day of the Lord's glory comes through the day of small things. We endure the day of small things by looking and longing for that great day of glory when Christ returns. To do this, we need to avoid seeking importance in the fleeting fruit of numbers, finances, buildings, or reputation, but instead, trust in the Holy Spirit and walk in step with him. So, what does that look like in a rural church?

Local Importance: Is Not This the Carpenter's Son?

One way to consider this would be to assess the local importance of our ministry. No one outside our region or county might have heard of our town, let alone our church, but we matter in our village. A rural pastor and church committed to their town can serve meaningfully, making it an essential part. This often comes naturally to a small church in a small place. The church family is embedded in their community, working and playing locally. Christians who long to share the gospel will probably find it natural to get involved in village clubs and societies.

We see this in our church. When the village toddler group closed, a group of moms from the church offered to keep it going. When we purchased the building, it was a natural decision to share space with the local tearoom and offer offices that local businesses could rent. The income we receive from this is essential in repaying building loans, but the sense that the church is part of the community and working together for the general good of the village is just as important.

All churches seek to be rooted and involved in their communities. The more static nature of rural communities and the smaller numbers of people make this easier for rural churches. To be part of the community is essential to our mission. Even though they were only in Thessalonica briefly, the missionaries Paul, Silas, and Timothy wrote that they "were ready to share with you not only the gospel of God but also our own selves" (1 Thess 2:8).

This desire to share ourselves and God's gospel comes from an understanding of God's character. God views love as necessary. People matter to our Lord, and we conform to the likeness of Christ when we treat people with love as essential bearers of the divine image. As we treat people well as individuals and, by extension, seek to serve our communities, caring for the least and the outcast, enriching village life, and bearing more than our share of local responsibility, then our church can become an essential part of local life.

The Downside of Having a Reputation

A downside to this local visibility also exists. When we are seen favorably, it makes the church important to the town and helps us to share the gospel openly. However, if we gain a bad reputation, this can be much harder to shift. Sometimes, a church deserves a bad reputation, having acted in a legalistic manner or taken a judgmental attitude to some matter in the village in the past. If this is the case, all we can do is seek to humbly live in love and service of others so that the reputation is no longer deserved, and neighbors might be pleasantly surprised.

A more difficult situation is when the church acquires a bad reputation for doing the right thing. I heard of a church locally seen by the village as unpatriotic and even traitorous for conducting a marriage shortly after the Second World War. The marriage was between a local woman and a German airman who had been a prisoner of war, barracked on a farm near the village. They were both Christians and met during the war. Afterward, they wanted to get married. The church knew how unpopular it would make them, but saw that they were brothers and sisters in Christ, who were both members of the church. They knew that in Christ, all are one. And so they married this couple, and their reputation was destroyed.

It must have been tempting to find a reason not to conduct the wedding! They must have known the price they would pay. We might well face the same dilemma. As we seek to serve the local community and build up a good reputation, we might need to take a side in village disputes, and we will judge, hopefully, as best we can by Christ's standards. These might not always be the popular ones! We know that the truth can cost us dearly.

I wonder, though, whether that little church, which saw deeper than nationality, into the heart of an "enemy" pilot and welcomed him as a brother into their church family, might have become a place where outcasts knew they were welcome. If Jesus could welcome this man, maybe there is room at his table for them. Jesus was ridiculed by the religious leaders of his day as "a glutton and a drunkard, a friend of tax collectors and sinners" (Matt 11:19). He was neither a glutton nor a drunkard. Yet he was a friend of tax collectors and sinners, and the disdain of the Pharisees was a source of comfort to them.

Jesus acquired a double reputation. If you were good and self-righteous, he would never meet your standards. If you were bad and self-aware, you might risk coming near. Maybe you might hope that you would find welcome and forgiveness from such a king as this. Perhaps you could wet his feet with your tears and wipe them with your hair. Isn't that just what we did, figuratively, when we first came to him as broken sinners?

The Timescales of a Village

In addition to being easy to lose, another problem with seeking local importance as a church is the slow, meandering pace of time in rural areas. The pace of farming life is much slower than the market-driven or industrial life of the big cities. Where the stock exchange trader hustles to buy one moment and sell the next, the farmer is shading his eyes against the sun as he reads the weather. Seasons of sowing and harvest, gestation, and growth call for patience and hard work. While farming is now not the major employer it once was in rural areas, it still profoundly influences rural culture.

Villages have long memories. Where we live, local people are used to seeing government initiatives come and go. They are accustomed to seeing the same with church plants as well. For years after the Lord planted our church, there was a clear sense that people were waiting to see if we would be around in a few years. Once we bought a building in the village, it became clear that people were prepared to take us more seriously. We had invested in bricks and mortar. We were committed to staying there. In our former church, in a city, we never owned a building, and no one noticed!

Time moves slowly in a village. People are happy to wait. This means that it might take years, probably decades, for a church to achieve even local importance. This is challenging for a church family, and even more so for a pastor. We like to make our mark, create a splash, and see changes made. We hope that this new initiative, the mission we run, or the program we start will be the talk of the town. When that is greeted with a sense of, "Well, we'll just see how it goes, pastor," it knocks the wind out of our sails.

The only way to enjoy a ministry of local importance is through years of selfless service. A village may notice a thirty-year ministry; the pastor certainly will. He will notice it in the stiff knees, constant tiredness, and personal cost. If he has not learned a deep dependence on his Father, he will notice it in his bitterness and the bitterness of his wife and children.

For just as the village says, "Just wait and see" to the church, so it says the same to the pastor.

Village Lad or Outsider—Neither Is Easy!

If you are a local man, then that brings its challenges. Jesus knows them well. The astonishment that greeted his preaching in the synagogue at Nazareth, his hometown, soon turned to scorn.

> They . . . said, "Where did this man get this wisdom and these mighty works? Is not this the carpenter's son? Is not his mother called Mary? And are not his brothers James and Joseph and Simon and Judas? And are not all his sisters with us? Where then did this man get all these things?" And they took offense at him. (Matt 13:54–57)

You can imagine the jibes: "Who does he think he is!" or "Get back to fixing tables, Jesus, and leave the preaching to your elders!" When you are known in a place, it is hard to shake that reputation. Seeking to preach to them is seen as putting oneself above others. And yet, it can be even worse not to be local! I know that, however much I love rural Norfolk and however deep my desire is for the salvation of my neighbors and their good, I will always be an outsider.

Rural folk do not move as much. Life is measured in seasons. Farming is talked about in generations. The rural church knows this. We slow down, count the cost, and keep going. We turn to our Father in trust and dependence yet again. Often, we are at the end of ourselves, tired and in danger of being weary in doing good, and yet the Spirit once again gives hope, faith, love, and peace. This slow and steady progress, this turning of the years, this need to set our hand to the plow and not look back is costly. The temptation is to look for the quick fix, yet God's answer, perhaps the source of eternal importance in rural ministry, is not to go quicker but slower.

Eternal Importance: Building with Gold, Silver, and Precious Stones

We might long for results in weeks, and the village might look to years, but the Ancient of Days works over centuries. The Lord's perspective is eternal; whether considering a day or a thousand years, he works quickly and slowly, moving in both in the same way (2 Pet 3:8).

This means we do not know what will be important. The span of a human life is far too short a time to measure importance. If we can understand the incredible patience of our Lord in working out his purposes, we can be free to do what he has set before us, trusting that he will make it important as he sees fit and in his good time.

Esther, Mordecai, and Shimei

In the book of Esther, we find this amazing story of the Lord saving his exiled people through Esther and Mordecai, but often we read past their ancestry. In Esth 2:5–7, we read,

> Now there was a Jew in Susa the citadel whose name was Mordecai, the son of Jair, son of Shimei, son of Kish, a Benjaminite, who had been carried away from Jerusalem among the captives carried away with Jeconiah king of Judah, whom Nebuchadnezzar king of Babylon had carried away. He was bringing up Hadassah, that is, Esther, the daughter of his uncle, for she had neither father nor mother. (ESV)

Esther and Mordecai are descendants of Shimei. It was this Shimei who cursed King David as he was fleeing Jerusalem with a few loyal followers in the face of a rebellion led by his son Absalom. Abishai, one of David's commanders, wanted to kill Shimei for this, but David prevented him. Later, when David defeated Absalom and was restored to his throne, he again showed mercy to Shimei and forgave him (see 2 Sam 16–19).

We do not know if Shimei had his children before he cursed David. Yet imagine if David had exacted judgment on him and he had died childless. Or if David, in common with many rulers, had decided to avenge himself on Shimei and his family. Then there would have been no Mordecai or Esther.

David did the right thing; he acted mercifully, just as he had received mercy from the Lord. David made a godly decision. If you read through 2 Samuel, this mercy to Shimei might impress you, but it does not strike you as a particularly significant event in David's reign. Yet the Lord then used the descendants of Shimei to save his people from destruction in the days of the Persian Empire. David's act of mercy is seen in its full importance only six hundred years afterward!

Ruth and Boaz

Similarly, there was a godly farmer called Boaz. He had taught his servants to fear the Lord, so when a Moabite refugee asked to glean on the edges of his field, the foreman among Boaz's harvesters let her. Boaz then treated Ruth and his mother-in-law, Naomi, with godly kindness. Ruth's faithfulness to Naomi and the Lord saved them from hunger and Naomi from despair. It also impressed Boaz; he undertook the full and holy duty of a kinsman redeemer in marrying Ruth and providing her and Naomi with the security, home, and family such a marriage gives.

When we read the book of Ruth, we are struck by Ruth's amazing faithfulness to the Lord and then by Boaz's ongoing, godly attitude in his words and behavior. Theirs is a story of love for the Lord, love for others, and finally, the love of marriage. Ruth is a refugee; Boaz is a farmer. They live their lives in fear of the Lord and faithfulness toward him. Then you come to the last few verses of the book:

> Now these are the generations of Perez: Perez fathered Hezron, Hezron fathered Ram, Ram fathered Amminadab, Amminadab fathered Nahshon, Nahshon fathered Salmon, Salmon fathered Boaz, Boaz fathered Obed, Obed fathered Jesse, and Jesse fathered David. (Ruth 4:18–21)

Three generations after the simple faithfulness of Ruth and Boaz, David is born. This faithfulness is one of the most important relationships in the Bible, yet it is only seen after three generations. Indeed, as important as King David was, the true importance of Ruth and Boaz's ministry is seen more than a thousand years later. Both Boaz and Ruth are mentioned in Matthew's great genealogy of Jesus Christ (Matt 1:5).

God Sees the End from the Beginning

This is how we come to understand the importance of rural ministry in the character of God. Our Father likes to work out his beautiful plans and loving purposes over many years, decades, centuries, and even millennia. The importance of our ministry will be revealed over many years and will be fully understood only when Christ returns and all things are revealed. This is freedom.

God sees the end from the beginning, and we do not unless he declares it to us (Isa 46:10). We are eternal beings. So we long to know the end too. Still, we cannot (Eccl 3:11). God has declared the end to us, in that his Son will return to judge the nations, raise the dead, and bring in the new creation when the world will be filled with the knowledge of the Lord as the waters cover the sea (Isa 11:9). He has not declared to us, though, the end of our ministries. We do not know how they are essential, and we cannot know, for our lives are too short.

Far from leaving us in despair, though, this leaves us living in shining hope. We do not know why our ministries are essential, and we are freed from trying to establish some fleeting importance now. We are free to pursue a ministry that we know will be eternally important because God has told us what it looks like to do so. God does not tell us the outcome of our work, but he tells us what he will use to bring about his purpose: obedient love.

Love: The Ministry of Eternal Importance

It is that simple. The ministry of eternal importance is love. It is the decades-long, back-breaking, perplexing, exhausting, humbling ministry of loving people so that we preach the gospel to them, serve them with all we are and have, and keep doing so until the Lord returns or calls us home. If Christ delays, I hope to be buried in the churchyard in my village, preaching Christ to the end. That will require a mighty work of the Spirit for a sinner like me, but he is a mighty Spirit full of kindness and grace.

A vital ministry is simply to labor at our allotted tasks in our allotted fields as farmhands. As Paul writes,

> I planted, Apollos watered, but God gave the growth. So, neither he who plants nor he who waters is anything, but only God who gives the growth. He who plants and he who waters are one, and each will receive his wages according to his labor. For we are God's fellow workers. You are God's field, God's building. According to the grace of God given to me, like a skilled master builder, I laid a foundation, and someone else is building upon it. Let each one take care how he builds upon it. For no one can lay a foundation other than that which is laid, which is Jesus Christ. Now, if anyone builds on the foundation with gold, silver, precious stones, wood, hay, straw—each one's work will become manifest, for the Day will disclose it because it will be revealed by fire, and the fire will test what sort of work each one has done. (1 Cor 3:6–13)

We are the farmers. Yet it is God who gives the growth. He will determine the harvest. Our wages are according to our labor and not the size of the harvest. We can enjoy giving ourselves in love to our brothers and sisters, as well as to our neighbors. We can trust the eternal importance of our work to a good Father and a kind Lord of the Harvest.

We do so knowing that if we build with gold, silver, and precious stones, our ministry will have eternal significance (1 Cor 3:10–14). It will be important because we build with love, the truth of the gospel, faithful Bible teaching, and sacrificial living, even though we keep doing the same things! Like the farmer, we sow and reap, year after year, and Jesus gives life through our undramatic ministry.

Thus, our ministry is essential because of the Lord's work in and through us, not because of tangible results. We can give thanks for visible results without depending on or unduly seeking them. We can keep our hand to the plow, trusting the Lord of the Harvest. To grasp this theology is utterly liberating, for it frees us to serve Christ as his love compels us and to rest well at the end of the day, content that our ministry is essential in God's sight and that he will reveal how when he sees fit.

12

How Do We Overcome Discouragement in Rural Ministry?

J. Matthew Shamblin

I honestly couldn't believe what I was hearing. As I walked down the aisle during the final prayer to greet worshippers as they exited, in hushed but ardent tones, the deacon forcibly told me that it was preaching like what I had just done that was behind the local head football coach's vow to never return to the church. The sermon was "too long" and "too preachy." Never mind the explanation of the biblical text. Forget the application of the text to the lives of the hearers. Who cares that many in the packed sanctuary indicated a response to the preached word? As a guest preacher, I was experiencing what the former pastor had endured for over six years. I now understand why he even refused to unpack his office during his entire tenure. It was evident why he always seemed to be in despair. He was under attack by the very ones who should have been his support system. The unfortunate reality is that the above story is true.

The Undeniable Difficulty of Rural Ministry

Let's admit that rural ministry can be very difficult. Even in the most populated rural areas, people are leaving. While other areas of the country are experiencing growth, the population of many rural areas is declining.[1] As would be expected, the worship facilities built during a population boom are now looking bare, with some even abandoned, and pastors are often blamed for this. Even if the modest church attendance represents a larger percentage of the community population than it ever has, in the eyes of some, the empty pews must be the pastor's fault.

Rural pastors are challenged not only by the declining population but also by the fact that the communities they serve are aging.[2] The growing, thriving congregations spoken of by the experts typically are not those served by rural pastors. In many cases, rural congregations are populated by long-established members who have been part of the church for decades. When a new pastor is brought to the church, he is expected to lead the church into the future, to reach new families, and to breathe new life into the congregation without changing a thing; of course, no one dares utter this Creed of the Established, but the new pastor is confronted with this unspoken tenant of dying faith when even the slightest deviation from the entrenched norm is attempted.

Rural churches often find themselves, not longing for the past that was, but for a past that never was. Admittedly, one of my favorite television shows is *The Andy Griffith Show.*[3] It was a show about an idealistic town nestled in the Piedmont foothills of North Carolina. It was a community that was a wonderful mixture of Appalachian and Southern culture. The characters always responded to the minor challenges they faced with some homespun ingenuity and laughter. No challenge was so big that it couldn't be resolved in less than thirty minutes.

The only problem was that Mayberry wasn't a real place, Andy wasn't a real sheriff, and there was never a real Barney who carried his bullet in his shirt pocket. It wasn't real. It didn't even portray reality as it was when it was filmed. There wasn't a single mention of the Vietnam War, racial tensions, government corruption, or antiwar protests. It reflected a time that never was. Many rural pastors face the challenges of a pastor that never was. Sure, the great pastor from long ago was used mightily by God; no one desires to deny that, but he was a man with feet of clay. He wasn't a perfect man; he would have indeed never claimed to be, but often, his legend looms far larger than the reality of who he was. God used him in his time, but often,

1. Associated, "Appalachian Counties."
2. Cohen and Greaney, "Aging in Rural Communities."
3. Leonard, *Andy Griffith Show*.

those who insist on keeping the legend of the past ever before our eyes can prevent a clear view of what God is doing in the present. The past must inspire us into the future, not discount what is happening today. Pastors often try to lead churches to be faithful today, but those churches refuse to move past yesterday.

The Need for a Pastoral Theology Grounded in a Right Understanding of God

"God has not forgotten you." I remember hearing my friend say these words in a phone conversation as I walked through the messy Dollar General Store. They helped. The fact that I needed to hear them uncovered a reality I didn't like to admit: my theology reflected a God who made mistakes. I deserved better, and I was at that place in my ministry by mistake, the mistake of God. Even as I write these words, it's embarrassing.

The God of the Bible doesn't make mistakes. This doesn't mean I always understand what he is doing or how all the pieces fit together. It does mean that a biblically rooted understanding of God does not portray God as mistaken, even with me, even during the most difficult of times, even when I don't like what I am experiencing.

As he prepared the second generation of people out of Egypt to enter the promised land, Moses assured them that God didn't have them wandering in the wilderness by mistake. Moses wrote, "For I will proclaim the name of the Lord; ascribe greatness to our God! The Rock, his work is perfect, for all his ways are justice. A God of faithfulness and without iniquity, just and upright is he" (Deut 32:3–4 ESV). There it is. God's ways are "perfect." God doesn't make mistakes. Even when the Hebrew people were wandering in the wilderness, they were there because God was faithful, even when they were not.

Years removed from that conversation with my friend, I can see why I was in that difficult ministry situation: I needed it because God is faithful even when I am not. That opposition I faced, those trials that came almost daily, and the pain I experienced revealed that, when I was squeezed, I believed God makes mistakes, that he doesn't give his children his best, and he isn't faithful. By accusing God, the attitude of my heart was blatantly revealed.

As a Christian and especially as a pastor, I must believe the clear teachings of the Bible, even when I can't put all the pieces together; this is faith. I must act on what I know about God, not what I don't know. I must trust in who God is, as revealed in the Bible, not imagined through my experiences. A faithful Christian must understand his circumstances through theology deeply rooted in the Scriptures, not the Scriptures through his circumstances. Admittedly, this is much easier said than done.

The Haunting Nature of Faithfulness

There is something simple about faithfulness. Not far from my house is a park I have driven past on many occasions, but I had only ever seen the sign. On a particularly difficult day, we needed a brief family getaway. We grabbed some fast food and headed up the hill into the park to find a place to have a little picnic. After we ate, we walked a little farther up the hill to a trail that overlooked the town. It overlooked two towns. One of the towns was large for a rural community, and the other was easily passed by. In the smaller of the two towns, I could see the small church. I knew the church because I knew the pastor. Unlike many pastors, he chose to stay; I mean, he really stayed. He has faithfully served that church for more than fifty years. He has been there since the babies were born. He laid the elderly to rest. He has preached the Bible. He has prayed. He has carried out his pastoral duties faithfully. He began his service there all those years ago as a young man, and now he is an old man. He is an inspiration. He has just kept going. When we look at the pages of Scripture, Daniel was one of those guys. He was faithful. Daniel was told, "But go your way till the end. And you shall rest and shall stand in your allotted place at the end of the days" (Dan 12:13). Daniel began as a young man, being faithful in his generation, and now, after the visions and God has delivered him from certain death, what is he told? He is said to keep going and be faithful until the end; then, his faithfulness will be recognized. There is something hauntingly simple about faithfulness.

The difficult days reveal our theology in more ways than one. Those furnace experiences solidify our theology with life. It's not that we need those experiences so our theology will be true, but rather, through those experiences, our lives become a living example of just how true our theology is. When temptation entices us to give up, the only thing that keeps us going is the work of God. Paul writes, "And I am sure of this, that he who began a good work in you will bring it to completion at the day of Jesus Christ" (Phil 1:6). Paul's confidence wasn't in people; his confidence was in God.

Rural places are often hard places. Rural life is not an easy life. It is a life of do-it-yourselfers who live far away from the bustle and the convenience of urban sprawl. The difficulties of rural living have led these individuals to rely solely on themselves to get things done. My wife's grandfather was one of these plainspoken men. Louie had been diagnosed with terminal cancer, and he was near the end of his life. Louie had been a lifelong alcoholic; he lived with his common-law wife and, in his final days, was just as loud and boisterous as ever. I'll never forget the scene: his hospital bed was in the living room where he could watch TV and greet those who came to see him. On this day, we planned a time for me to be alone with him. I intended to share the gospel. As I started the conversation with him, as I had with many people before, he gruffly interrupted me and said, "Matt, do you see something wrong with me?" The words that came out of my mouth almost startled me: "Yeah, Louie, I do." "What is it?" he asked. That forthrightness opened the door for me to explain to him that he was a sinner and that he needed a Savior. Out of that gruff conversation, I had the opportunity to lead him to faith in Jesus Christ. Louie was a hard man. He communicated clearly and simply, and it was in that same way he responded to faith in Christ, clearly and simply.

God doesn't just call the pastor to the church, but he also calls the church to the pastor. A God who doesn't make mistakes must then, by necessity, bring a pastor to a difficult place to bring him to the end of himself and, by grace, give him strength. The difficulty of the circumstances of rural ministry does not come by chance to those called to rural ministry; it is God's best for that pastor, at least for a time. Lauded pastor Charles H. Spurgeon writes, "Remember this, had any other condition been better for you than the one in which you are, divine love would have put you there."[4] God only gives the best to his children. That conversation with my friend showed me I was mistaken about God, and I was mistaken about me. That simple statement, "God has not forgotten you," revealed my pride. I believed that I deserved better than God's best for me. It was hard for me to imagine that God had put me in a difficult place, not by mistake but on purpose, for him to address the issue of pride in me. God used that difficulty to teach me about himself and to teach me about myself. That rural place brought me to the end of myself, and there I was met by the grace of God. God strengthens us in our weakness by his grace.

4. See Spurgeon, "Morning and Evening."

What Keeps Us Going Is What Got Us There in the First Place

God's call on one's life has power. The apostle Paul responded to the leading of the Holy Spirit to refrain from preaching the gospel in Asia, as the Holy Spirit was leading him to minister in Macedonia, ultimately resulting in the gospel reaching Europe. Luke writes,

> And they went through the region of Phrygia and Galatia, having been forbidden by the Holy Spirit to speak the word in Asia. And when they had come up to Mysia, they attempted to go into Bithynia, but the Spirit of Jesus did not allow them. So, passing by Mysia, they went down to Troas. And a vision appeared to Paul in the night: a man of Macedonia was standing there, urging him and saying, "Come over to Macedonia and help us." And when Paul had seen the vision, immediately we sought to go on into Macedonia, concluding that God had called us to preach the gospel to them. (Acts 16:6–10).

Paul responded to the call of God on the road to Damascus and the call of God to go to Macedonia. It was his surety in the leading of the Holy Spirit that gave him the boldness to minister in difficult places.

The Basis of Our Calling

The call of ministry comes by the will of God. Charles Spurgeon offers such timeless wisdom to his readers in all his published works. His insight into pastoral ministry has become legendary, particularly when it concerns the call of God. He famously said to his students,

> "Do not enter the ministry *if you can help it*," was the deeply sage advice of a divine to one who sought his judgment. If any student in this room could be content to be a newspaper editor, or a grocer, or a farmer, or a doctor, or a lawyer, or a senator, or a king, in the name of heaven and earth let him go his way; he is not the man in whom dwells the Spirit of God in its fulness, for a man so filled with God would utterly weary of any pursuit but that for which his inmost soul pants.[5]

5. Spurgeon, *Lectures to My Students*, 23.

The Prince of Preachers poignantly emphasizes how God works within a person to instill an unyielding desire to serve their Savior. This desire is given to him by the Holy Spirit, and it is a desire for which he was created.

The call to ministry comes out of the will of God. Paul writes, "For by grace [we] have been saved through faith. And this is not of [our] own doing; it is the gift of God, not a result of works, so that no one may boast. For we are his workmanship, created in Christ Jesus for good works, which God prepared beforehand, that we should walk in them" (Eph 2:8–10). It is a call for which we were created before time. Our response to that call is just like that of the apostle Paul responding to the leading of the Holy Spirit to go to Macedonia; it is something that we must do because it is why we were created.

The call of God can seem clear when things are going well. When attendance is up and the waters of baptism are flowing, the call can be self-affirming. However, when times are tough, doubt can creep in. It is during the tough times, brothers, that we must remember how assured we were of the call of God. When we sensed the moving of the Holy Spirit, and we surrendered to his will, we must return there, knowing that God does not change.

The Significance of Our Calling

The God who doesn't change also calls us to a ministry better than we deserve. The call of God is a call that comes by his grace. God is using us in pastoral ministry, but God is using pastoral ministry in us. God uses the ministry in our formation into Christlikeness. This means even the difficult times come out of God's grace for us. God is giving us better than we deserve to shape us into what we could never have been through our ability. Dave Earley writes, "I define and describe the call to church ministry as an inner conviction from God confirmed by the church, verified by giftedness, and supported by results. It is an unmistakable sense that I have been summoned by the Lord to lifelong vocational service in building his church."[6] The call to pastoral ministry comes out of the will of God. This call was impressed on us by the work of the Holy Spirit. He has summoned, and we have responded. By grace, God is not only using us in the lives of others, but he is using others in our lives, too. Our response to God's call is only one step in his ongoing preparation of us for his service. Even while we serve, we are still a work in progress. Times may become difficult, but remember, God has allowed even the most challenging times to produce

6. Earley, *Pastoral Leadership*, 22.

Christlikeness in us. Brothers, we must keep returning to the reality that the call of God is why he made us and what he has called us, and it is better than we truly deserve.

What Keeps Us Going Is Found in How We Lead

Leaders often have the kind of personalities where they take charge no matter the circumstances. After spending some time in leadership, it can often be freeing not to be in charge. I have found vacations extremely freeing, but it might not be for the reasons you think. My primary job during vacations is to drive where I'm told. My wife is a planner. Once we agree on a destination, everything but the driving is up to her, and boy, does she take it seriously. She plans the hotels. She organizes and packs the items we will need for the trip. Once we have arrived, she knows exactly what we will do each day. It is wonderful! I am along for a well-planned ride. Leaders often have the personalities to make things happen, but ministry doesn't work that way. If we can make it all happen in our power, why do we need God?

The One We Follow Determines How We Lead—His Character

Ministry is far more about who we are following than it is about where we are leading. If we know the One we follow, we cannot go wrong with where we are going. Ministry is more about followership than leadership. Just as our response to difficulty reveals what we believe about God, so, too, does our approach to ministry leadership. If we believe everything depends on our ability to make it happen, then not only are we going to live stressed-out, anxiety-ridden lives, but we're ultimately leading in a way that misrepresents God. Wasn't it Jesus who said, "Come to me, all who labor and are heavy laden, and I will give you rest. Take my yoke upon you, and learn from me, for I am gentle and lowly in heart, and you will find rest for your souls. For my yoke is easy, and my burden is light" (Matt 11:28–30)? Doesn't the invitation of Jesus also include ministry leaders? It especially includes ministry leaders. The way we lead reveals to those we lead what we genuinely believe about God. Our perfectionism, short temper, laziness, and even anger can misrepresent God and his mission through us.

One of the most robust sections in any bookstore is the section that deals with leadership. It appears these days that anyone famous in any field writes on leadership. The temptation is to adopt popular leadership theory within the local church. God has not called us to lead as a celebrity chef, football coach, or Navy SEAL. God has called us to "shepherd the flock of God that is among us" (1 Pet 5:2). What we believe about God is evident not just in what we say but even more so in how we live and, yes, in how we lead. Portraying a correct view of God in how we lead is deeply convicting, but even in that, we must remember that he is a God of grace.

God's word is sufficient in revealing God, and he has not left us alone in leading and shepherding others in ministry. Wayne Grudem writes, "The sufficiency of Scripture means that Scripture contained all the words of God He intended his people to have at each stage of redemptive history, and that it now contains all the words of God we need for salvation, for trusting Him perfectly, and for obeying Him perfectly."[7] We must not tell others of the sufficiency of Scripture in knowing the God who saves and then lead them to believe his shepherding of them through us somehow comes by the employment of methods that contradict his character. Our actions, especially through leadership, tell others what we really believe about God.

Some stories of leadership are just beyond belief, and when they come from one who has been entrusted to shepherd the flock of God, they can be unthinkable. Stories of pastors pitting one faction of the church against another, utilizing the pulpit to publicly embarrass or address private matters, or even using pastoral influence to slander members of the congregation to diminish their impact, are not only sinful but, above all, misrepresent God. Lording over others not only misrepresents God, but it also misrepresents how God works in light of the cross and the empty tomb.

Guilt or public pressure is not even a cheap replacement for the transforming power of the Holy Spirit. Ministry can be discouraging, but we cannot succumb to the shortcut of utilizing worldly powers to produce a change in the human heart. God's promise through the new covenant is a promise that couldn't be produced through the old covenant, a promise of regeneration.

> I will take you from the nations and gather you from all the countries and bring you into your own land. I will sprinkle clean water on you, and you shall be clean from all your uncleanliness, and from all your idols I will cleanse you. And I will give you a new heart, and a new spirit I will put within you. And I will remove the heart of stone from your flesh and give you a heart of flesh. And I

7. Grudem, *Systematic Theology*, 127.

> will put my Spirit within you, and cause you to walk in my statutes and be careful to obey my rules. You shall dwell in the land that I gave to your fathers, and you shall be my people, and I will be your God. (Ezek 36:24–28)

The new covenant is distinctly different from the old covenant because it brings about change from the inside out, not the outside in. Our leadership either portrays a leadership dependent on this new covenant transformation or a reversion to an old covenant methodology that ultimately ignores the intervention of God in time through Jesus Christ's death, burial, and resurrection. God brings about a change in those difficult members of our congregation the same way he brought about a change in us, divinely.

As much as we may want, we cannot bring about change in others. Ministering to people week after week can be so discouraging when we cannot see any change. Again, we must be taken back to our theological moorings. God has not called us to bring about change in others; only the Holy Spirit can change people. A ministry that is rooted in the word and is carried out through the word has the assurance that God will accomplish what he intends to accomplish (Isa 55:10). Keep going and be found faithful. God has entrusted his people to us. He has not left us alone, and he has not left them alone. He works in ways that we cannot see. Continue to minister through the word and leave the changing of us and others to him.

Following the Chief Shepherd—Hearing His Voice

Leading faithfully in ministry is not only about accurately displaying the character of God through our leadership as we follow him. It is about being sensitive enough to the voice of the Holy Spirit that we are led where he would have us go. Jesus spoke of the difference the Holy Spirit would make in the lives of his followers when the Spirit came. John writes, "When the Spirit of truth comes, he will guide you into all the truth, for he will not speak on his own authority, but whatever he hears he will speak, and he will declare to you the things that are to come" (John 16:13). The disciples had the expectation given to them by Jesus that they were not to figure out what God wanted them to do on their own but through the work of the Holy Spirit. D. A. Carson writes,

> The verb used here and repeated in vv. 14, 15 (*anangellō*, NIV "tell" in v. 13, and "make known" in vv. 14, 15) suggests an announcement, indeed in this context a revelatory declaration (as its

> use in 4:25 suggests), but it is a *reiterative* announcement (Brown, 2. 708). These features square best with the view that *what is yet to come* refers to all that transpires *in consequence* of the pivotal revelation bound up with Jesus' person, ministry, death, resurrection, and exaltation. This includes the Paraclete's own witness to Jesus, his ministry to the world (16:8–11) primarily through the church (15:26, 27), and the pattern of life and obedience under the inbreaking kingdom, up to and including the consummation. All of this the Spirit of truth "announces," yet in making it known, he is doing little more than fleshing out the implications of God's triumphant self-disclosure in the person and work of his Son.[8]

If the church's primary business is to make Jesus known among the nations, then this will be done by the work of the Spirit through the church. The ministry leader must be sensitive to the leadership of the Holy Spirit and obey his voice. In the Gospel of John, Jesus assured his followers of the coming ministry of the Holy Spirit. This assurance comes in the context of encouragement. Jesus was going away, but the Holy Spirit would never leave the disciples alone. They would have the Holy Spirit to enable their ministry and encourage them in it; it presupposes that times would not always be easy.

We never know what God is doing in the lives of those in the churches we serve. If we are assured that God is leading us, that we are hearing his voice, then we must be assured that the same Holy Spirit is also preparing the way by leading others. Paul writes, "For in one Spirit we were all baptized into one body—Jews or Greeks, slaves or free—and all were made to drink of one Spirit. For the body does not consist of one member but of many" (1 Cor 12:13–14). We know what God is doing in the church we serve depends not on us but on the Holy Spirit. He uses us out of his grace. During difficult times, we must not succumb to the temptation to believe it's all up to us. The Holy Spirit joins and knits together the church, and rest assured, the rural church is not too far off the beaten path for it to go unnoticed by Satan. Satan will sow in tares among the wheat, but we know God has not left us alone in spiritual warfare. The same Spirit that works in us is at work in others, and he is at work to unite the church in the mission God has given her.

8. Carson, *Gospel According to John*, 540–41.

He Leads Us Together

The word *orphan* immediately suggests vulnerability. The imagery of orphans and adoption is utilized in biblical literature to invoke these images to portray what God has done for us in salvation. In vulnerability and helplessness, God, in his mercy, has called you out of death into the safety of life with him as Father. Because of what Jesus Christ has done, we are no longer on our own to deliver ourselves. Yet when we read the words of Jesus, he refers to more than delivering us from an eternity separated from him, but also the Spirit's guidance of his followers today.

> And I will ask the Father, and he will give you another Helper, to be with you forever, even the Spirit of truth, whom the world cannot receive because it neither sees him nor knows him. You know him, for he dwells with you and will be in you. I will not leave you as orphans; I will come to you. Yet a little while and the world will see me no more, but you will see me. Because I live, you also will live. In that day you will know that I am in my Father, and you in me, and I in you. Whoever has my commandments and keeps them, he it is who loves me. And he who loves me will be loved by my Father, and I will love him and manifest myself to him. (John 14:16–21)

The Helper, the Holy Spirit, was given to enable and empower obedience. It was the same Holy Spirit who called us to salvation and called us to serve in rural ministry. He will enable our obedience. He will sustain us, and he will empower us when we are ready to give up. We are not orphans, forgotten by our Father, but are tenderly loved children on whom our Father lavishes his very best on us and those we serve.

Although I believe the primary text for Christian leadership is the Bible, we can learn from secular leadership insofar as it doesn't contradict or take precedence over what is taught in the Bible. While completing the research for my dissertation, I uncovered something very encouraging. For pastors, the members of our congregations rate our leadership better than we do.[9] This research was conducted in a rural setting and considered education, as well as employment status (vocational/bivocational). Often, the pastor is his greatest critic. There are, of course, exceptions to every piece of research and every opinion. The research demonstrated that from the

9. See Shamblin, *Leadership Perceptions.*

congregation's perspective, they generally think more of your leadership than you do!

The ministry that exists to please people is a dangerous one. If our motivation is to garner the applause of others, then we will undoubtedly be set askew from the mission given to the church and the faithful approach to leadership demonstrated by Jesus. Ultimately, we are not called to build a megachurch, have a plethora of social media followers, or be famous. We are called to be faithful to God and his calling on our lives.

Conclusion

Life tells the tale. What is revealed through life is often not what we wish were revealed. The calling of God on the life of a pastor is essential. A deep conviction that the pastor is doing what God himself has called him to do keeps him rooted in the ministry and his place of service. The way we approach ministry tells the tale. If we believe God controls what he is doing in us, we must acknowledge this includes the place we serve. How we lead others tells the tale if we believe the Bible is sufficient in revealing God and his directions on how to follow him as he leads others. God has not called us to a church, even in the rural places, and forgotten us; he has us there on purpose. Some may say, "God has called you there because he knew you could handle it. He knew it would take someone tough." However, we find in the Bible that perhaps God has called us to serve in rural areas because we are weak. We are prone to giving up. We are prone to walking away, but we don't. The Holy Spirit has prevented us from making a mess of the Lord's church, our families, and our lives because when we are weak, then he is strong. He helps us not in our strengths but in our weaknesses.

13

How Do We Minister Within the Context of Our Limitations?

Kevin Blackwell

But we have this treasure in clay jars, so that it may be made clear that this extraordinary power belongs to God and does not come from us.
2 Corinthians 4:7

This book has aimed to assist rural pastors in theologically bridging their pastoral work with the community and the people they serve. The hope is also to encourage co-vocational pastors to think theologically about the scope and nature of an infinite God. I hope you will see how an infinite God can transform and change all your finite perceptions of your local ministry context.

I primarily work with small-town, rural, co-vocational pastors. I have dedicated most of my work to training, equipping, and encouraging small-town, small-church, co-vocational ministers. These faithful shepherds have become my heroes as I watch them serve, often with limited resources, living out God's calling on their lives. This is mainly done without any notoriety, denominational awards, invitations to speak at events, or public recognition. All pastoral ministries have challenges, but the struggles of co-vocational ministry are unique due to the limitations of time, resources, training, and isolation. All ministry contexts have limitations, but the rural pastor is naturally aware of these more than most serving in ministry. Co-vocational pastors have similar responsibilities to their full-time colleagues. They are expected to prepare sermons weekly, visit members, plan events, counsel people through crises, mediate conflicts, and manage the budget, all while finding time to minister to their families and work a full-time job (or two). While the scope of the pastoral task is the same, these tasks are often performed under extreme limitations of time and resources. It is no wonder that many of these pastors feel overburdened.

With the decline in church attendance in North America, the need for pastors to serve co-vocationally will continue to increase. Twenty years ago, 45 percent of churches in America had fewer than one hundred attendees; today, that number has grown to 65 percent.[1] Even deep in the heart of the Bible belt, the Alabama Baptist Convention has noted that 54 percent of its churches have a co-vocational pastor. If you count Alabama Baptist churches that have staff members who are co-vocational, the percentage would be closer to 90 percent.[2] These statistics suggest that future church ministry will be increasingly co-vocational. Co-vocational ministry is not a new concept.

For centuries, church leaders have served the body of Christ while working a trade. The apostle Paul worked as a tentmaker to support his ministry. He reminds the Thessalonians of his work as to not depend on the church to support him: "For you remember, brethren, our labor and toil; for laboring night and day, that we might not be a burden to any of you, we preached to you the gospel of God" (1 Thess 2:9). Acts 18:3 also speaks of his work as a tentmaker with Priscilla and Aquila as they served together in Corinth.

The idea of professional ministers serving full-time in the church was not fully realized until the 1950s as American evangelicalism embraced this new paradigm. Seminary education also became more critical as these full-time ministers were expected to have a full-time ministry and theological education as a qualifier to serve. This shift to full-time professional ministers unintentionally created a sectarian culture within North American evangelicalism, in which those who served full-time in ministry were perceived as more capable or astute than those who served in part-time roles.

1. Earls, "Small Churches Continue Growing."

2. Alabama Baptist, "Bivocational Ministers," para. 4.

Whether spoken or not, a feeling emerged that those who served part-time in ministry were not gifted enough to serve the church full-time. Much like baseball has players in the major and minor leagues, the thought prevailed in ecclesiastical circles that if one applied and dedicated himself aptly, he would be called up to the big leagues. I sense this type of sectarian thinking is changing in the North American ecclesial landscape, and it is a welcomed shift. Removing the stigma of co-vocational ministry is long overdue.

Serving an Unlimited God with Limited Resources

In 2020, I began serving in a co-vocational role as a teaching pastor at the church my family and I were attending. I have long appreciated the service of those who serve the church while maintaining a full-time job, but rarely served in this role. This new opportunity, however, has given me a new perspective and a greater empathy with those serving in co-vocational roles. I was not prepared for the challenges that would come as I quickly learned the need to balance the demands of a full-time job, family, and my staff position responsibilities. I write this chapter as a person living the co-vocational experience—not as an advisor but as a practitioner. I also find myself in need of encouragement more now than I did when I was serving in a full-time ministry role. With the changing ministry paradigms in pastoral leadership, never has it been a more critical time to encourage those serving in co-vocational roles.

The greatest threat to co-vocational pastors is the temptation to focus on the limitations inherent in small churches and part-time roles; however, these should not define their calling. The highest calling is to focus on the opportunities for disciple-making gospel impact in the communities they serve and not on the limitations. The size of your ministry and your town are not the most important things; it is the size of the God you serve and his ability to do the impossible. Often, those serving in ministry can forget this basic theological concept when they are surrounded by discouragement, limitations, and struggles. Your church might have limited resources, but God does not. Your church might not have the technology you desire, the nicest facilities, the large budget, or the preferred location. Still, it does have access to the indwelling and inexhaustible power of the Holy Spirit.

What your church lacks in resources is not nearly as important as the imbued, unlimited power available through the presence of God. The same God who saved you, called you, and sent you now dwells with you and empowers you to fulfill the mission he has called you to, regardless of the limitations of your ministry context. If we are not careful, we may be inclined to believe that full-time pastors receive the fullest measure of God's power, and co-vocational ministers somehow receive a limited portion. No one I know would verbalize this thought, but maybe internally, you are dwelling on limitations so much that the limitless power of God is being realized in half-measure. We would do well to remember Paul's prayer for the church at Ephesus:

> I do not cease to give thanks for you, remembering you in my prayers, that the God of our Lord Jesus Christ, the Father of glory, may give you a spirit of wisdom and of revelation in the knowledge of him, having the eyes of your hearts enlightened, that you may know what is the hope to which he has called you, what are the riches of his glorious inheritance in the saints, and what is the immeasurable greatness of his power in us who believe, according to the working of his great might which he accomplished in Christ when he raised him from the dead and made him sit at his right hand in the heavenly places, far above all rule and authority and power and dominion, and above every name that is named, not only in this age but also in that which is to come; and he has put all things under his feet and has made him the head over all things for the church, which is his body, the fulness of him who fills all in all. (Eph 1:16–23)

We have a hopeful calling, a rich inheritance, and a power in us that is immeasurable, though we often allow our weaknesses and struggles to diminish these wonderful truths. How does the co-vocational pastor balance what he knows to be theologically accurate with the everyday realities of limitations and weakness? The answer may surprise you—I encourage you to embrace your weaknesses and limitations. We will never truly know the full power of God at work within us and our ministries unless we first come to grips with and even embrace our weaknesses and limitations.

I know this is a countercultural mindset, but in God's economy, embracing human weakness is to understand his power at work within us fully. Paul certainly experienced this in his own life and ministry. He speaks often about his sinfulness (1 Tim 1:15), his zealous past (Phil 3:8), his many burdens (2 Cor 11), his loneliness in ministry (2 Tim 4:10–11), and his trust in religious piety (Phil 3:6–7). Paul embraced the fact that he was a "clay jar." He states, "But we have this treasure in clay jars, so that it may be made clear that this extraordinary power belongs to God and does not come from us" (2 Cor 4:7). The power of the gospel at work in Paul was the treasure. Paul's repudiation of himself as a clay jar is not an expression of false humility. He recognizes that earthen vessels are, by nature, fragile, inferior, and easily broken. Paul saw himself as an ordinary, weak object containing a valuable and powerful treasure, which was the foundation for his effectiveness.

A key aspect of Pauline thought is the recognition of weakness and the embracing of the fragility of his life so that the contents within the jar are viewed as most important. No one in their right mind would depend on the strength of a clay jar, nor would they be overwhelmed with its beauty. It is only a container, and its weakness illuminates the greater treasure contained within its fragility. As Paul asked Christ for the removal of a perceived weakness in 2 Cor 12:7–10, the response of Christ gives us insight into why Paul was a consummate embracer of weakness. Jesus said to him, "My grace is sufficient for you, for power is made perfect in weakness." Paul's response has echoed through the ages: "So, I will boast all the more gladly of my weaknesses, so that the power of Christ may dwell in me" (2 Cor 12:9). When we, like Paul, fully embrace our weakness, we realize our only hope is the power of God, which works best in our weakness. This is an excellent reminder for the pastor serving a small church with limited resources, asking himself, "How in the world can this church ever be all that God desires it to be?" The strength of a church is never found in its pastor, its members, or its resources. All those things are clay jars. The hope of every church, regardless of size, is found in the power of Christ, which dwells within the members and ministers who collectively serve together.

God has a long history of making a significant impact through what some consider weakness. We often make the mistake of conflating weakness with smallness, but it is not so with God. In Judg 7, God won a victory over thousands of Midianites through Gideon's three hundred. God intentionally dwindled the number of warriors to defeat the large army so that the glory for the victory would be his and not in the strength of the warriors. The gospel went forth to the nations through a small group of uneducated disciples who lacked material resources yet fully embraced the power of God. Some of the most theologically enduring books of the Bible were not written in palaces or temples but in prison cells and deserted islands. In the economy of God, the things the world considers foolish and inadequate (clay jars), when entirely consecrated and dedicated, can change the world and have an amazing impact. I hope every co-vocational, small-church, rural pastor understands that, though you might lack resources, you are resourced bountifully with the treasure of the power of God within you.

The Calling to Make Disciples Where God Has Placed You

The calling of a co-vocational pastor will never be more or less than making disciples where God has placed him. You may be co-vocational at church, but you are called to be a full-time pastor who makes disciples. Even with limited resources, you have all you need to fulfill the role of a disciple-making minister. The minimum for church ministry is the Great Commission of our Lord in Matt 28:18–20:

> And Jesus came and said to them, "All authority in heaven and on earth has been given to me. Go therefore and make disciples of all nations, baptizing them in the name of the Father and of the Son and of the Holy Spirit, and teaching them to obey everything that I have commanded you. And remember, I am with you always, to the end of the age."

This Commission is for everyone who knows Jesus as Savior. It is the guiding commission of churches in large urban areas and small rural communities, and is the ubiquitous calling for everyone in ministry. Ultimately, the success of our ministries will not be found in the size of our churches but in how faithful we are to make disciples and equip others to do the same. Unlike other church programs requiring money, dozens of volunteers, and hours, making disciples who make disciples can be accomplished in a context of limited resources. If you have a heart for Christ, a good handle on God's word, and at least one person needing discipling, then you have all you need to be a disciple-making minister. It is important to remember that the gospel spread to the uttermost parts of the world through disciple-making multiplication. It spread among men who were co-vocational, lacking formal theological education, and had no church buildings, funds, or curriculum to distribute their teachings. Although they had limited resources, they were promised the presence of God (Matt 28:20; Acts 1:8), and they had a burning passion to share the good news of Jesus with others (Acts 4:20).

The words of Matt 28:18 are of super importance if you are to fulfill your role as a disciple-making pastor in your context. In this verse, Jesus declares, "All authority has been given to me in heaven and on earth." It is hard to argue with that statement, considering he had been dead in the grave a few weeks before. The word translated as "authority," *exousia*, means a delegated or conferred authority.[3] His authority was given to him by his Father. He was given authority over death, hell, sin, disease, the earthly realm, and the spiritual realm (Phil 2:10). That authority was exceptional, unprecedented, and unparalleled. Still, the most amazing thing is what happens next.

Notice the transition from verse 18 to verse 19, "Go therefore." The word "therefore" is Christ imparting his authority to the disciples. Jesus essentially says, "I have taught you; I have shown you; I have led you, and all authority belongs to me; therefore, I am passing it on to you." They were not commissioned to go under their power and influence a few people. This statement is critical in understanding the Commission of Jesus to his church. Jesus has the authority, and he has given it to you to go in his name to make disciples.

Luke shares in Acts 1 that Jesus also said not only would they have authority to go, but they would be empowered to be effective. "But when the Holy Spirit has come upon you, you will receive power and will tell people about me everywhere" (Acts 1:8). And to make sure that you understand the hand off taking place, notice Matt 28:20, "And be sure of this: I am with you always, even to the end of the age." That authority would be signified by his presence, which is being promised in perpetuity. The Commission given to the disciples has been handed down to you regardless of where you serve or your ministry status. The delegated authority given to the disciples, given to Paul, Silas, Martin Luther, George Whitefield, William Carey, and Billy Graham has also been given to you.

Within the Great Commission of Jesus, the church finds a distinct imperative command replicating his process of making disciples. The command is clear: "make disciples." The imperative active verb "make disciples" (*mathēteusate*) has three verb participles: go, baptize, and teach, which modify the command.[4]

The highly effective pastor places a priority on making disciples through going, baptizing, and teaching. The common denominator of each of these activities is the power of relationships. With the limited time a co-vocational pastor has, he must prioritize disciple-making relationships. This involves two aspects. The first is establishing disciple-making relationships

3. Bible Hub, "exousia."

4. Bible Hub, "mathéteuó."

within the local church context. At The Station Church,[5] where I serve as the teaching pastor, I have seen the power of forming disciple-making relationships with the people in my ministry context. As I began my ministry at the church, I found it crucial to establish these types of relationships with the small-group leaders within my church. For twenty-one weeks, I met with these leaders in an intimate, closed discipling format. By closed, I mean once we started meeting, I didn't ask others to join our huddle. I wanted the opportunity to focus on these leaders for an extended period, meeting weekly to read Scripture and equip them in the areas of identity in Christ, intimacy with Christ, instruction from Christ, and making an impact for Christ.[6]

This began an incredible movement within our church, where these small-group leaders began pulling others aside for discipling, just as I had discipled them. We are still seeing the remarkable fruit of this each week, as a large percentage of our membership has been personally discipled by another member. It was life-giving and organic, and it multiplies exponentially the number of people in the church who have been prepared to make disciples in their family, at work, and in their areas of influence.

This introduces the second aspect of disciple-making relationships as discipled church members begin reaching their community to make disciples. David Platt reminds us,

> The plan of Christ is not dependent on having the right programs or hiring the right professionals, but on building and being the right people—a community of people—who realize that we are all enabled and equipped to carry out the purpose of God for our lives.[7]

Building a disciple-making culture within the local church enables this missional response. By now, you are likely thinking of why you can't do similar things in your context, but I want to remind you of two things. First, regardless of the size of your context, disciple-making multiplication can occur. Jesus began a worldwide movement with twelve men and has empowered you to do the same.

Second, despite your lack of resources and time, relational disciple making must be a priority. In my co-vocational context, I disciple people

5. For more information about our church, go to www.thestationchurch.org.

6. I have published my disciple-making tool, co-authored with Dr. Randy Norris, which I hope will be a good resource for you: *Cultivate Disciplemaking: Growing Disciples Who Make Disciples*. It is available through Amazon or Cultivatedisciplemaking.com.

7. Platt, *Radical*, 92.

using one hour per week. This small investment of time will bring huge dividends to your ministry. You do not need a large church, lovely buildings, a huge budget, or a large surrounding population to begin a disciple-making revolution; you need to start with the commitment to disciple someone. The process begins in the heart of a pastor who loves God and people, loves God's word, and has one hour per week to pass the Great Commission torch to those in the church and the community.

The church's work is to make disciples who make disciples, and church leaders must share this vision as the one true mission. If church leaders are not themselves disciple makers, it is hard to imagine that church members and ministries will follow the process of Jesus and be obedient to the Great Commission. The most Jesus-like activity that a pastor can accomplish is to invest in a few with the expectation of replication and multiplication. This investment will not involve announcements in the bulletin or sign-up sheets, but rather a personal invitation to journey together in becoming mature followers of Jesus. This relational investment will likely result in disciples reaching their culture through a missional disciple-making lifestyle. Craig Etheredge reminds church leaders of the exhilaration of missional disciple making,

> There is nothing more satisfying in ministry than making disciples. Record attendances come and go. Large events come and go. Building projects and mission trips come and go. But the one thing that will satisfy you in ministry is pouring your life into a few people and watching them do the same thing.[8]

When it is all said and done, your ministry will not be defined by how many people were in your church, how big your budgets were, or how many people enjoyed your sermons. The effectiveness of your ministry is found in how many multiplying disciple makers you have cultivated. You have all the tools you need to accomplish this task.

A Word of Encouragement

The goal of this chapter is to remind you that through the empowering of the Holy Spirit, you have all you need to be an effective disciple-making pastor. God has called you to serve where you are, and if he has called you there, he has gifted and equipped you to serve effectively. Don't give in to

8. Etheredge, *Bold Moves*, 215.

the temptation to focus primarily on jars of clay at the expense of missing the treasure enclosed within. Spend time today taking inventory, not of the resources you don't have, but of the ones you do have. Find a network of fellow co-laborers and share burdens, ask God for a fresh vision to reach your community, and tell someone about Jesus today. Wins in ministry are sometimes not publicly seen but often come in hundreds of ways that might seem insignificant at first but, over time, yield fruit. If you serve faithfully within the smallness of your context, God will bring about huge results in the lives of those you are called to serve.

I recognize, however, that some of you reading this book are in a difficult season of ministry. You are in good company. Paul would have certainly understood the difficulties you are facing. In 2 Cor 11, Paul offers a long list of his ministry difficulties. In this list, he mentions several events that impacted him physically, but verses 28 and 29 are distinctly different, and I believe he saves his greatest burden for last. He states, "Then, besides all this, I have the daily burden of my concern for all the churches. Who is weak without my feeling that weakness? Who is led astray, and I do not burn with anger?" (NLT).

Paul states in verse 28 that his burden for the church, the people he was called to serve, is a daily burden. The physical burdens of Paul, stemming from the previously mentioned events in the chapter—shipwrecks, beatings, and imprisonments—would eventually heal, but the burden for the church was daily, literally moment by moment. His ministry with people, particularly the Corinthians, involved entering their weaknesses and feeling the pain of every person, especially those who had fallen away. He equates this to having his soul burned, "Who is led astray, and I do not burn with anger?" Notice he uses the term *burden*; some translations say "pressure." The word Paul uses suggests a hostile banding together or stacking up of pressures and burdens. The issues of the church were coming at him as hostilities that were banding together and building upon his soul.

The word for "concern" is the same word used in other Scriptures for worry and anxiety. It is a word that means to be fractured or divided into parts. Paul speaks here of the seriousness of the burdens placed on him through ministry. According to Paul's words, the burdens were beginning to compile, and as they stacked against him, they were crushing him into pieces. The burdens and pressures of dealing with broken people can break your heart into pieces.

With this in mind, let's talk about ministry burdens. A burden is not necessarily a bad thing; some are God-given. For example, Nehemiah was given a burden by God to rebuild the walls of Jerusalem. The prophets Nahum, Habakkuk, and Malachi all begin their prophecies with "The oracle [also translated as burden] of the word of the Lord." If God calls you and you do not have a deep, soul-shaking burden for the work that you are in, there is something amiss. Pastors should have a burden for people, cities, and communities, and a burden to see these people saved and discipled. A burden is necessary before any great work of God can be accomplished. The reason so many churches are dying in North America is mostly because hundreds of congregations have lost their burden for the unsaved in their communities. The problem comes when a pastor's God-given burden becomes a burden. Maybe that describes your current ministry condition—your burden has become an overwhelming load. Here are a few simple biblical reminders to lessen your burden.

God has placed in your heart an irrevocable calling. No matter how bad things seem or how low you feel, the calling of God on your life is not impacted or lessened during difficult days. I was told early on in ministry that rough days would come when I would need to hold on to my calling a little tighter than usual. Out of the billions, God has called a few to do what you do. It is the highest privilege known to man. In speaking of his ministry, Paul says to the Corinthians, "For it is the God who said, 'Let light shine out of darkness,' who has shone in our hearts to give the light of the knowledge of the glory of God in the face of Jesus Christ" (2 Cor 4:6).

In the fourth chapter of 2 Corinthians, Paul is reflecting on the purpose and passion of his call to ministry. He compares his calling to a light shining in his heart, which is likened to the moment God called light out of darkness at creation. Paul states that his ministry calling includes the same glory that is shown on the face of Christ at the transfiguration! "So we do not lose heart. Even though our outer nature is wasting away, our inner nature is being renewed day by day. For this slight momentary affliction is preparing us for an eternal weight of glory beyond all measure" (2 Cor 4:16–17). The surpassing glory of God, which empowered Paul's calling, was glorious enough to overcome the worst of his situations. Though you might be fatigued, your mind exhausted, and your spirit crushed, the calling in your heart is as glorious as the first light of creation and the face of Christ on Mount Hermon.

God will one day place on your head an incorruptible crown. "And when the Great Shepherd appears, you will receive a crown of never-ending glory and honor" (1 Pet 5:4). Peter looks to the day our Great Shepherd presents you with a crown of glory. Many crowns are mentioned in Scripture, but this one is reserved explicitly for faithful pastors. I know you have days when your head is spinning with tasks and others when your head is overwhelmed with burdens. Yet, I can guarantee a day is coming when your head will be crowned with glory. Pastor, do not lose heart. One day in eternity, the very one whom you have preached about, prayed to, and spoken of will take those nail-scarred hands and place a crown on your head. You have preached about his glory, but one day, he will share it with you.

Conclusion

Finding Security in a Changing World

Jeff Clark

The Greek philosopher Heraclitus is credited with saying, "Change is the only constant in life." Looking at the tremendous changes over the last sixty-plus years of my life, Heraclitus was undoubtedly correct.

When I was growing up in southern middle Tennessee in the 1960s and 1970s, we had two pieces of electronic technology in our house: a rotary phone and a black-and-white television with a thirteen-inch screen. By 1976, we had a touch-tone telephone in the house due to an uncle who was an early computer programmer. He said one day, all phones would be touch-tone.

The advances are astounding if we look at the technological changes that have occurred just within my lifetime. From rotary phones and black-and-white televisions to cell phones with 5G capabilities, the internet in the palm of our hand, and now the burgeoning world of Artificial Intelligence (AI), technology is transforming how we perceive our world today.

Changes coming today are having a profound impact on daily life. These changes come from every facet of life faster than most churches and pastors can handle. For example, the radical changes brought about by the COVID-19 pandemic have been staggering. Five years ago, who knew what Zoom was or who had ever heard of Facebook Live? Since the pandemic, the number of people who have dropped out of church has been stunning, not to mention the new way to do the Lord's Supper and take up the offering. And the changes keep coming!

In today's world, these rapid changes are not just happening in far-off cities like New York, Los Angeles, or Chicago. Rural areas are experiencing changes at a pace never before seen. For instance, a pastor trying to keep up with the changes in communication styles can be overwhelmed. Older people in a rural church may enjoy a phone call or a home visit. Baby boomers and millennials may communicate through text messages and use Facebook as their primary social media platform. For Gen Z, these outdated forms of communication are for old people. They use Snapchat and TikTok as their social media platform of choice. And by the publication of this book, I am sure another social media platform will sweep through North America's middle and high schools.

This is just a look at social media platforms. The rapid changes in sexuality, Christian deconstructionism, and the wide acceptance of AI technology affect even the most rural areas of North America. The changes occurring in the more rural regions today can easily cause a pastor to despair.

Scripture is filled with change. The garden of Eden did not last three chapters. Satan soon came to the garden and tempted Adam and Eve with the most powerful temptation of all: "For God knows that when you eat of it your eyes will be opened, and you will be like God, knowing good and evil" (Gen 3:5 ESV). Oh, to be like God! To be his equal and to be free of his commands. Finally, Adam and Eve could chart their course. Their decision to alter God's plan for their life ultimately led to a disaster that continues to affect humanity to this day.

Since the garden of Eden, humanity has tried to get a handle on change. Throughout history, humans have feared change and tried to limit its impact on daily life. Scripture is replete with men and women who were called to change: Moses was called to change his vocation. Peter was called to change his dietary rules and his perspective on gentiles. And Paul was called to change his theology and career. Often, these changes came in opposition to the one being changed. Moses asked God to send Aaron in his place, Peter told God he could never eat anything unclean, and Paul was on his way to destroy the Christian church when his life was turned upside down.

We must be clear at this point. We serve a God that requires change in us, but he does not change. He does not adapt to the changing times. He remains persistent in his requirements and does not compromise to accommodate extenuating circumstances.

In the drifting tides of change engulfing the church today, we must be reminded of God's unchanging nature. This chaotic world we live in today presents the church pastor with many challenges. The temptation to compromise theologically to be seen as "relevant" or to be perceived as successful is a powerful one, and many churches are succumbing to it today.

How do we make sure we are not compromising our theology in how we do church today? We must return to the one source that guides Christians in theology and practice. We return to the Bible. When we look at our circumstances first rather than Scripture, it is easy to compromise Scripture to be seen as acceptable to today's culture. However, if we are going to have a solid foundation in this time of rapid change, we must examine once again what the Bible says about God and his unchanging nature. From Scripture, we find our footing to face the chaotic world we live in today.

Review of Scripture

Scripture is replete with references to God's unchanging nature. In this section, we will examine just two texts for two reasons. First, for most readers of this book, little evidence is needed to believe in the unchanging nature of God. Most Christians already believe in God's immutability. The second reason for using only two texts is for the sake of brevity. With these two things in mind, two texts should suffice.

The first text is found in Num 23:19 where Balaam, the prophet, has been called by Balak to curse the Israelites. Here, Balaam proclaims in a poem,

> God is not a man, that he might lie,
> or a son of man, that he might change his mind.
> Does he speak and not act,
> or promise and not fulfill?

Balaam states in this text that God is not like a man. He cannot lie, he does not change his mind, and he does not make a promise he cannot fulfill.

Dennis Cole, in his volume in The New American Commentary series, describes God as,

> Different and separate from mankind, transcendent beyond the realm of humanity with all of its tendencies toward falsehood, deceit, misfortune, and calamity. Therefore, he does not need to

> repent of any moral or ethical turpitude or misdeed. God is immutable, and His word bespeaks His incomparable integrity.[1]

Ultimately, the three characteristics concerning the unchanging nature of God found in this verse have much to say to us today. First, God cannot, nor will he lie. Whatever he says is the absolute truth. This means he does not deceive people, and what he says is entirely trustworthy. Furthermore, he does not say one thing today, only to say another thing later. This would, in its essence, be a lie, and Scripture is clear: God does not lie.

Second, God does not change his mind. He does not think one thing one day and then change his mind later. His thoughts are always the same, always consistent.

If God does not change his mind, the question arises as to the efficacy of prayer. If we cannot change God's mind, then why pray? R. C. Sproul responds to this question by stating,

> First of all, we pray because he commands us to pray. Second of all, through the instrument of prayer, we enter into communion and dialogue with our heavenly Father. It is an unspeakable privilege to be able to pray and to let him know our burdens and what's on our minds. He knows what we're going to ask before we ask it, and yet he encourages us to ask him, not for His benefit, but for ours.[2]

Third, God does not make a promise he does not or will not fulfill. In other words, if God says he will do something, you can "take it to the bank." He has never failed on even one of his promises, both for blessings and judgment. Our problem is that God does not work on our timetable. Thus, what looks like God not fulfilling his promise is simply God's timing. In a world that likes instant results—instant potatoes, 5G internet, and instant gratification—God's timing is often difficult to understand. One old pastor said years ago, "God's timing is seldom early, but he is never late."

This means every promise God makes in the Bible that has yet to be fulfilled certainly will be fulfilled at some point in the future. We do not have to wonder if; we can only wonder when. For example, we can know that Jesus will return one day. We can only ponder the timing. Knowing that he keeps his promises offers peace in chaotic situations.

The second verse we need to examine is Heb 13:8, which states, "Jesus Christ is the same yesterday and today and forever." This text is often

1. Cole, *Numbers*, 200.
2. Sproul, "Can Our Prayers," para. 2.

quoted without reference to the surrounding verses. While the verse can certainly stand on its own and means precisely what it says, greater depth can be gleaned by putting it in context with the verses immediately before and after it. Immediately preceding verse 8, the writer states in verse 7 to remember what the original church leaders taught them. Remember how these teachers lived and the outcome of their way of life. The challenge in Heb 13 is for the readers to imitate the faith of these original teachers. Following verse 8, verse 9 challenges the readers of Hebrews not to be led away by strange teachings but to be strengthened by grace. The gospel is not "grace plus." Instead, the gospel is "grace alone."

The recipients of the book of Hebrews were facing new "teachers" coming into the fellowship with new ideas. Ideas that were different and not what they learned from the leaders at the beginning. These new teachers were teaching new rules about dietary laws in addition to the grace taught by the original leaders.

Thus, the writer's challenge to the readers of Hebrews is to remain faithful to the teaching they had received from their original leaders. A teaching focused on grace alone. They were not to be led away by adding rules and regulations to what they had heard.

The fantastic part of this text is verse 8, which comes in the middle of this argument. The writer is stating that Jesus Christ is the same yesterday, today, and forever. This simple statement confirms multiple gospel truths. First, Jesus is eternal. For him to be the same, he had to exist yesterday, today, and forever. He has been from the creation of the world, he exists today, and he will live forever.

Because Jesus is eternal, he is part of the Godhead. His preexistence proves his divinity. What can be said about Jesus can be said about God the Father, for they are one. Thus, if Jesus is the same yesterday, today, and forever, God is the same yesterday, today, and forever.

The writer of Hebrews was trying to tell his readers that nothing has changed concerning the gospel. What the readers learned from the original leaders has not changed. In essence, the new "teachers," who were teaching grace plus dietary laws, were teaching something new, different, and contrary to the apostles' teachings.

The message of the cross has not changed over the last two thousand years. The offense of the cross cannot be adapted to fit different cultures or changing times. Jesus came to save sinners by dying on the cross and being raised from the dead. We must never be allowed to say Christianity contains "Jesus plus" or "Jesus minus" anything.

A Review of God's Characteristics

God's characteristics confirm his unchanging nature. He cannot have conflicting attributes. What is true about one aspect of God confirms other aspects of his nature.

The first of these confirming characteristics comes from the text in Hebrews, confirming that God is eternal. He existed yesterday. He exists today. And he will exist forever. While the Bible is filled with references to God being infinite, Rev 1:8 sums it up best when it says, "'I am the Alpha and the Omega,' says the Lord God, who is and who was and who is to come, the Almighty."

Because God is eternal, he can't change his mind. Changing one's mind can only take place within the confines of time. To change one's mind, there must first be a time when one has an idea. Later, they changed their mind about the original idea. Since God is the same yesterday, today, and forever, and since he is not bound by time, he can't have an idea at a point in time and then, at a later point in time, change his mind about that idea.

The second characteristic of God that confirms his unchanging nature is that God is perfect. Matthew 5:48 states it this way: "You therefore must be perfect, as your heavenly Father is perfect" (ESV). Deuteronomy 32:4 expands on Matthew's brief statement by stating,

> The Rock, his work is perfect,
> for all his ways are justice.
> A God of faithfulness and without iniquity,
> just and upright is he.

Since God is perfect, he can't change his mind. To change one's mind implies that something better or worse must take place. Since God is perfect, he cannot change for the better.[3] This means God only makes one decision concerning a situation or an idea, and his decision is always perfect. God cannot change his perfect mind to make a more perfect decision later. He cannot become "perfect-er." This also means that God does not agonize over making decisions. He does not wring his hands over a situation or a decision. His decisions are immediate, perfect, and unchanging.

3. Got Questions, "Immutability of God."

Third, God is omniscient and all-knowing, so he cannot change his mind. In 1 John 3:20, he states this truth straightforwardly when he says, "For whenever our heart condemns us, God is greater than our heart, and he knows everything" (ESV). Simply put, God knows everything. There is nothing God does not already know. Thus, when you pray, you are not informing God of something he did not know. Instead, you are sharing with him the burden of your heart about a situation he already knows.

Thus, for God to change his mind would mean he learned something new and made a decision to change.[4] Changing one's mind requires new knowledge that precipitates the change. Because of his omniscience, God cannot change his mind. There is nothing more for him to know.

Implications

It is clear from Scripture that God does not change, does not compromise, nor does he adapt to fit the current situation. He is the one constant in a world that is constantly changing. God is the one exception to Heraclitus's statement concerning change.

In our world today, where change is bombarding us from every angle, what are the implications of God's immutability? Does God's unchanging nature have anything to do with a rural church? The answer to these questions is emphatically YES. Our entire Christian faith is based on the immutability of God. The Christian church is built on God's unchanging promises.

The implications may seem obvious, but we must remember them as we struggle to adapt to a new world. First and foremost, the God of the Bible is the same God we serve today. J. I. Packer states it this way:

> God does not change with the times, nor does he adapt to current situations. Where is the sense of distance and difference, then, between believers in Bible times and ourselves? It is excluded. On what grounds? On the grounds that God does not change. Fellowship with Him, trust in His word, living by faith, and "standing on the promises of God," are essentially the same realities for us today as they were for Old and New Testament believers. This thought brings comfort as we enter into the perplexities of each day: amid all the changes and uncertainties of life in a nuclear age, God and His Christ remain the same, almighty to save. However, the thought also presents a searching challenge. If our God is the same as the God of

4. Got Questions, "Immutability of God."

> New Testament believers, how can we justify ourselves in resting content with an experience of communion with Him, and a level of Christian conduct, that falls so far below theirs?[5]

The sameness of God throughout the generations is evidence that Christians did not make God up, nor did we make God in our likeness. He was, is, and always will be holy God. He is wholly different from man, the world, and changing times.

This means in our chaotic world we can lean on God for strength, support, guidance, and direction for our lives. He is from everlasting to everlasting.[6] We do not have to seek to reinvent God for a new generation, for he is the same as he has always been.

The irony here is that the unchanging God of the universe calls for his children to change constantly. The Bible contains stories of God's call to change for individuals and the church. A few examples of God calling for dramatic change, previously referenced in this chapter, include Adam and Eve, Abraham, Moses, Saul, David, the disciples, and Paul.

If we are surrounded by a world changing faster than we can keep up with, and God calls for us to change constantly, how can we trust in a God who never changes but calls for us to change? Because of his unchanging nature, we can trust his leading in this chaotic world. While he leads us to change how we do church, engage lost people, and change our personal lives, his constancy is the rock that provides us the strength and confidence to adapt to today's rapidly changing world.

The second implication of God's immutability is that he is the standard for our life and ministry. We do not make decisions based on current situations, our beliefs, or what is popular today. Instead, we make decisions based on the unchanging word of God and, more importantly, on the permanent nature of God.

We cannot trust ourselves or our culture to determine what we should do or be. Left to myself, I can make poor decisions, or at best, decisions at a point in time that do not stand the test of time. Also, left to myself, I have little authority to recommend change or to challenge the status quo. My track record of making decisions independently does not inspire confidence in those I lead. I must draw my authority from some source other than myself. I must turn to the one who has never changed throughout

5. Packer, *Knowing God*, 72

6. "Before the mountains were born, before you gave birth to the earth and the world, from eternity to eternity, you are God" (Ps 90:2).

eternity. The one who is always right, who never has to backtrack, whose decisions have withstood the test of time. I must turn to God as the standard for everything I do and appeal to him for every decision I make.

The third implication sets church leaders free once they truly grasp this idea. Because God is immutable, we are not called to woo the world to become believers in the gospel. Instead, we are called to proclaim the gospel to a lost and dying world faithfully. We are not called to lure people into the church with extravagant music, sermons with video and PowerPoint presentations, or with fancy lighting systems. (Please hear me now: I am not against quality worship. I am against using these things in place of the work of the Holy Spirit or to conjure up emotions to emulate the Holy Spirit's work.)

In our success-oriented world, churches can be tempted to equate success in church with numbers. Closely related to the infatuation with numbers comes the subtle temptation to compromise God's unchanging truths to obtain numerical success. Often, numerical success brings fame and recognition, but it never leads to a truly spirit-filled life change.

For those serving in rural areas, it is easy to feel jealous of others who have better resources and larger numbers. It is easy to wonder what it would be like to pastor a large, growing church in the suburbs.

Compromising to get people to attend church is a subtle but powerful temptation. We must be comfortable with proclaiming the truth without compromise and realize that this is success for the Christian pastor, regardless of the size of the church.

When using God as the standard, measuring success shifts to faithfulness to Scripture, unity within the church, and obedience in making disciples. If we promote something that comes from the character of God, we are faithful to the task God has entrusted to us, and we are leaning on God's unchanging character to build his church. Thus, we can be comfortable with the size of the church regardless of the numbers.

Conclusion

We live in a rapidly changing world, and the temptation to compromise to be relevant is real. We naturally want to be seen as successful. The only thing we can do in response to this temptation is to hold fast to God's unchanging word. This requires a ruthless examination of everything the church does to see if it complies with God's unchanging desire for the church. We must be willing to let go of sacred cows that do not advance the gospel or strengthen the flock. While this is easier said than done, it is the task of the pastor and church leaders to lead the church to be more in line with God's character. Satan desires to distract the church with busy work that has no kingdom significance. We must be diligent to seek God in everything we do. After all, he is the standard by which we do everything.

One other word on the unchanging nature of God. He loves little churches! In Luke 12:32, Jesus states, "Don't be afraid, little flock, because your Father delights to give you the kingdom." The all-knowing, unchanging God who was, who is, and who is to come loves you and your little church. He knows where you are and challenges you as you look at today's chaotic times to not be afraid because it is his delight to give you his kingdom.

Let this sink into your soul for a minute! God delights to give you and your little church his kingdom. He delights in giving his kingdom to little churches in obscure places. You are not serving in the minor leagues. You are not serving in a starter church. You are serving exactly the people that the God of the universe has entrusted to you. Trusting in his unchanging nature provides solace and comfort when everything seems precariously on the edge of collapse. The promise he made over two thousand years ago is still true today: "On this rock I will build my church, and the gates of Hades will not overpower it" (Matt 16:18). If God is unchanging, we can rest in this promise. Because we can rest in this promise, we do not need to be afraid. The church belongs to him, and he has promised to protect it.

So, go forward in ministry and be bold. He is building the church, and he has not changed our task, nor has he forgotten a single child of his over the last two millenniums. He will certainly not forget you and your flock!

Bibliography

Adam, Peter. *Hearing God's Words: Exploring Biblical Spirituality*. Downers Grove, IL: InterVarsity, 2004.

Alabama Baptist State Board of Missions. "Bivocational Ministers." https://web.archive.org/web/20200511105512/https://alsbom.org/ministries/bivocational-ministers/.

America Counts Staff. "What Is Rural America? One in Five Americans Live in Rural Areas." United States Census Bureau, August 9, 2017. https://www.census.gov/library/stories/2017/08/rural-america.html.

Associated Press. "Appalachian Counties Suffer Biggest Population Losses, Census Finds." WYMT, August 12, 2021. https://www.wymt.com/2021/08/13/bell-county-suffers-largest-population-loss-state-census-finds/.

Becker, Jane S. *Selling Tradition: Appalachia and the Construction of an American Folk, 1930–1940*. Chapel Hill: University of North Carolina Press, 1998. https://archive.org/details/sellingtraditiono000beck/page/n4/mode/1up.

Bible Hub. "1849. exousia." https://biblehub.com/greek/1849.htm.

———. "3100. mathéteuó." https://biblehub.com/greek/3100.htm.

Blackaby, Henry T., and Claude V. King. *Experiencing God: Knowing and Doing the Will of God*. 15th ann. ed. Nashville: Broadman & Holman, 2004.

Blackwell, Kevin, and Randy Norris. *Cultivate Disciplemaking: Growing Disciples Who Make Disciples*. Birmingham: Make and Teach, 2022.

Bolsinger, Tod. *Canoeing the Mountains*. Downers Grove, IL: IVP, 2015.

Byrne, Francis., et al. *A Thirst for Land: A History of Scioto County, Ohio, and Greenup County, Kentucky*. Portsmouth, OH: Shawnee State University Press, 2004.

Carson, D. A. *The Gospel According to John*. The Pillar New Testament Commentary. Grand Rapids: Eerdmans, 1991.

Charnock, Stephen. *The Existence and Attributes of God*. 2 vols. Edited by Mark Jones. Wheaton, IL: Crossway, 2022.

Christian History Institute Editors. "The Life & Times of Jesus of Nazareth: Did You Know?" *Christian History* 59 (1998). https://christianhistoryinstitute.org/magazine/article/life-and times-of-jesus-did-you-know.

Clark, David K. *To Know and Love God*. Foundations of Evangelical Theology. Wheaton, IL: Crossway, 2003.

Clark, Jeff. "Rural Theology: A Brief Examination of Scripture from a Rural Perspective." Unpublished White Paper, 2004.

Clements, Andrea D. *The Trauma Informed Church: Walking with Others Toward Flourishing.* Johnson City, TN: Uplift, 2023.

Clifton, Mark. *Reclaiming Glory: Revitalizing Dying Churches.* Brentwood, TN: B&H, 2023.

Cohen, Steven A., and Mary L. Greaney. "Aging in Rural Communities." *Current Epidemiology Reports* 10 (2023) 1–16. https://link.springer.com/article/10.1007/s40471-022-00313-9.

Cole, R. Dennis. *Numbers.* The New American Commentary 3b. Nashville: B&H, 2000.

Cooper, Lamar Eugene. *Ezekiel.* The New American Commentary 17. Nashville: B&H, 1994.

Crossan, John Dominic, and Jonathan L. Reed. *Excavating Jesus: Beneath the Stones, Behind the Texts.* San Francisco: Harper San Francisco, 2002.

Crouch, Andy. *The Life We're Looking For: Reclaiming Relationship in a Technological World.* New York: Convergent, 2022.

Daman, Glenn. *Shepherding the Small Church.* Grand Rapids: Kregel, 2008.

Dunne, John Anthony. "Colossae." In *The Lexham Bible Dictionary*, edited by John D. Barry. Bellingham, WA: Lexham, 2016.

Earley, Dave. *Pastoral Leadership Is . . .: How to Shepherd God's People with Passion and Confidence.* Nashville: B&H Academic, 2012.

Earls, Aaron. "Small Churches Continue Growing—But in Number, Not Size." Lifeway Research, October 21, 2021. https://research.lifeway.com/2021/10/20/small-churches-continue-growing-but-in-number-not-size/.

Ellul, Jacques. *The Technological Society.* Translated by John Wilkinson. New York: Vintage, 1964.

Elmer, Duane. *Cross-Cultural Servanthood: Serving the World in Christlike Humility.* Downers Grove, IL: IVP, 2006.

Etheredge, Craig. *Bold Moves: Lead the Church to Live Like Jesus.* Colleyville, TX: DiscipleFIRST, 2016.

Frost, William G. "Our Contemporary Ancestors in the Southern Mountains." *The Atlantic Monthly* (1899) 311–19. https://babel.hathitrust.org/cgi/pt?id=hvd.hx4mp5&seq=7.

Garrett, Duane A. *Proverbs, Ecclesiastes, Song of Songs.* The New American Commentary 14. Nashville: B&H, 1993.

Got Questions. "What Is the Immutability of God?" https://www.gotquestions.org/immutability-God.html.

Green, Patricia, developer. *Christy.* TV series. The Rosenzweig Company and MTM Enterprises, 1994–95.

Griggs, Donnie. *Small Town Jesus: Taking the Gospel Mission Seriously in Seemingly Unimportant Places.* Damascus, MD: EverTruth, 2016.

Griggs, Donnie, and Ronnie Martin. *Pastoring Small Towns: Help and Hope for Those Ministering in Small Places.* Brentwood, TN: B&H, 2023.

Grudem, Wayne. *Systematic Theology: An Introduction to Biblical Doctrine.* Grand Rapids: Zondervan, 1994.

Grundmann, Walter. "δόκιμος." In *Theological Dictionary of the New Testament*, edited by Gerhard Kittel and Gerhard Friedrich, translated by Geoffrey W. Bromiley, 2:255. Grand Rapids: Eerdmans, 1964.

Hall, Jacquelyn Dowd, et al. *Like a Family: The Making of a Southern Cotton Mill World.* New York: Norton, 1987.

Hamilton, Victor P. "463 הָבַל." In *Theological Wordbook of the Old Testament*, edited by R. Laird Harris et al. Chicago: Moody, 1999.

Hanalis, Blanche, developer. *Little House on the Prairie*. Ed Friendly Productions, NBC Productions, 1974–83.

Heisler, Greg. *Spirit-Led Preaching: The Holy Spirit's Role in Sermon Preparation and Delivery*. Nashville: B&H Academic, 2007.

Henry, Matthew. *Matthew Henry's Commentary in One Volume*. Grand Rapids: Zondervan, 1961.

Hubbard, D. A. "Ethiopian Eunuch." In *New Bible Dictionary*, edited by D. R. W. Wood et al. 3rd ed. Downers Grove, IL: InterVarsity, 1996.

Hunter, James Davidson. *To Change the World: The Irony, Tragedy, & Possibility of Christianity in the Late Modern World*. New York: Oxford University Press, 2010.

Hurtado, Larry W. *God in New Testament Theology*. Nashville: Abingdon, 2010.

Jung, Shannon, et al. *Rural Ministry: The Shape of the Renewal to Come*. Nashville: Abingdon, 1998.

Kaiser, Walter C. *Ecclesiastes: Total Life*. Everyman's Bible Commentary. Chicago: Moody, 1979.

Keller, Timothy. *Center Church*. Grand Rapids: Zondervan, 2012.

———. *Why God Made Cities*. Adapted from the sermon "The Problem of the City," November 7, 1993. https://forcharlotte.org/wp-content/uploads/2016/12/Why-God-Made-Cities-Tim-Keller.pdf.

Kirchschlaeger, P. G. "Slavery and Early Christianity—A Reflection from a Human Rights Perspective." *Acta Theologica* 23 (2016) 66–93. https://doi.org/10.4314/actat.v23i1s.4.

Klassen, Ron, and John Koessler. *No Little Places: The Untapped Potential of the Small-Town Church*. Grand Rapids: Baker, 2017.

Koiter, Ian W. K. "Nazareth in the First Century." In *The Lexham Bible Dictionary*, edited by John D. Barry. Bellingham, WA: Lexham, 2016.

Laney, J. Carl. *Baker's Concise Bible Atlas: A Geographical Survey of Bible History*. Grand Rapids: Baker, 1988.

———. "Galilee." In *The Lexham Bible Dictionary*, edited by John D. Barry. Bellingham, WA: Lexham, 2016.

Leonard, Sheldon, creator. *The Andy Griffith Show*. TV series. Danny Thomas Enterprises, Mayberry Enterprises, and CBS Productions, 1960–68.

Lingenfelter, Sherwin, and Marvin Mayers. *Ministering Cross-Culturally: An Incarnational Model for Personal Relationships*. 2nd ed. Grand Rapids: Baker Academic, 2003.

Livermore, David. *Leading with Cultural Intelligence*. New York: Amacom, 2015.

Longenecker, Harold. *Building Town and Country Churches: A Practical Approach to the Revitalization of Churches*. Chicago: Moody, 1973.

Louw, Johannes P., and Eugene A Nida. *Greek-English Lexicon of the New Testament: Based on Semantic Domains*. 2nd ed. New York: United Bible Societies, 1989.

Luzbetak, Louis J. *The Church and Cultures: New Perspectives in Missiological Anthropology*. Maryknoll, NY: Orbis, 1998.

Maier, Paul L. *In the Fullness of Time: A Historian Looks at Christmas, Easter, and the Early Church*. Grand Rapids: Kregel, 1997.

Marshall, Catherine. *Christy*. New York: McGraw Hill, 1967.

Noble, Alan. *You Are Not Your Own: Belonging to God in an Inhuman World*. Downers Grove, IL: InterVarsity, 2021.

Oden, Thomas C. *The Living God*. San Francisco: Harper & Row, 1987.

Ohio Department of Health. *Preliminary Data Summary: Ohio Unintentional Drug Overdose Deaths*. Last updated January 3, 2023. https://odh.ohio.gov/wps/wcm/connect/gov/86452388-2e4b-48d6-a5e8-90ce24b30d0f/Ohio+Quarterly+Overdose+Report_Preliminary+Data_Q1_2023.pdf?MOD=AJPERES&CONVERT_TO=url&CACHEID=ROOTWORKSPACE.Z18_M1HGGIK0N0JO00QO9DDDDM3000-86452388-2e4b-48d6-a5e8-90ce24b30d0f-otRHmeH.

Packer, J. I. *Knowing God*. Downers Grove, IL: InterVarsity, 1973.

Parker, Kim, et al. "Demographic and Economic Trends in Urban, Suburban and Rural Communities." Pew Research Center, May 22, 2018. https://www.pewresearch.org/social-trends/2018/05/22/demographic-and-economic-trends-in-urban-suburban-and-rural-communities/.

Peterson, David G. *The Acts of the Apostles*. The Pillar New Testament Commentary. Grand Rapids: Eerdmans, 2009.

Platt, David. *Radical: Taking Back Your Faith from the American Dream*. Colorado Springs: Multnomah, 2011.

Plueddemann, James. *Leading Across Cultures: Effective Ministry and Mission in the Global Church*. Downers Grove, IL: IVP Academic, 2009.

Ramm, Bernard L. *Rapping About the Spirit*. Waco: Word, 1974.

Robinson, Thomas A. *Who Were the First Christians? Dismantling the Urban Thesis*. Oxford: Oxford University Press, 2017.

Root, Andrew. *The Children of Divorce: The Loss of Family as the Loss of Being*. Grand Rapids: Baker Academic, 2010.

Roth, Brad. *God's Country: Faith, Hope, and the Future of the Rural Church*. Harrisonburg, VA: Herald, 2017.

Sanneh, Lamin. *Translating the Message: The Missionary Impact on Culture*. Maryknoll, NY: Orbis, 2009.

Sawyer, M. James, and Daniel B. Wallace, eds. *Who's Afraid of the Holy Spirit? An Investigation into the Ministry of the Spirit of God Today*. Dallas: Biblical Studies, 2005.

Schermerhorn, John F., and Samuel J. Mills. *A Correct View of That Part of the United States Which Lies West of the Allegany Mountains, with Regard to Religion and Morals*. Hartford: Gleason, 1814. https://babel.hathitrust.org/cgi/pt?id=nyp.33433068187602&view=1up&seq=1.

Schulz, Charles M. *A Charlie Brown Christmas*. Lee Mendelson Film Productions, Bill Melendez Productions, 1965.

Shamblin, J. Matthew. *Leadership Perceptions: A Comparison of Pastors and Their Parishioners*. PhD diss., Tennessee Temple University, 2014.

Sproul, R. C. "Can Our Prayers Change God's Will? If Not, Why Pray?" Ligonier. https://learn.ligonier.org/qas/can-our-prayers-change-gods-will-if-not-why-pray.

Spurgeon, Charles H. "Despair Denounced and Grace Glorified." In vol. 28 of *The Metropolitan Tabernacle Pulpit Sermons*, 469–80. London: Passmore & Alabaster, 1882.

———. *Lectures to My Students: A Selection from Addresses Delivered to the Students of the Pastors' College, Metropolitan Tabernacle*. Vol. 1. London: Passmore & Alabaster, 1875.

———. "Morning & Evening: Evening Devo, Nov. 11th." Heartlight, November 11, 2025. https://www.heartlight.org/spurgeon/1111-pm.html.

Studd, C. T. "Only One Life, Twill Soon Be Past." Reasons for Hope* Jesus. https://reasonsforhopejesus.com/only-one-life-twill-soon-be-past-by-c-t-studd-1860-1931/.

Talmage, T. DeWitt. *The Pathway of Life*. New York: Christian Herald, 1894.

Tavernise, Sabrina, and Robert Gebeloff. "Once Rare in Rural America, Divorce Is Changing the Face of Its Families." *New York Times*, March 24, 2011. https://www.nytimes.com/2011/03/24/us/24divorce.html.

Thomas, Ian. *The Saving Life Of Christ*. Grand Rapids: Zondervan, 1961.

Wells, Barney, Martin Giese, and Ron Klassen. *Leading Through Change: Shepherding the Town and Country Church in a New Era*. St. Charles, IL: ChurchSmart Resources, 2005.

Wiersbe, Warren. *The Wiersbe Bible Commentary: The Complete Old Testament in One Volume*. Colorado Springs: Cook, 2007.

Winter, Ralph D., and Steven C. Hawthorne. *Perspectives on the World Christian Movement: The Notebook*. Pasadena: William Carey Library, 1999.

Witmer, Stephen. *A Big Gospel in Small Places: Why Ministry in Forgotten Communities Matters*. Downers Grove, IL: InterVarsity, 2019.

———. "Five Ways for Rural Ministry to Look Ahead." *Journal of Mid-America Baptist Theological Seminary* 8 (2021) 103–14. https://issuu.com/mabts/docs/mid-america_journal_2021-web.

Worldometer. "Countries in the World by Population (2023)." https://web.archive.org/web/20230829145320/https://www.worldometers.info/world-population/population-by-country/.

Wright N. T. *The Resurrection of the Son of God*. Minneapolis: Fortress, 1992.

www.ingramcontent.com/pod-product-compliance
Lightning Source LLC
LaVergne TN
LVHW050631100826
845148LV00011B/1833

* 9 7 9 8 3 8 5 2 6 8 2 9 0 *